PRAISE FOR
THE GREATEST ROMANCE

What a profound and applicable way to use this wonderful, yet often misunderstood, Old Testament book. Mrs. Welty was truly inspired by the Holy Spirit in this work. This ten-week journey will change your life and those who study with you. Thank you for creating such a wonderful devotional guide for all who follow and love Jesus.

— ***Dr. Charles Travis***, *President/Founder*
Aidan University, Logos Global Network
Jacksonville, Florida

Debbie Welty has written a thorough and inviting devotional study on one of the most misunderstood books in Scripture. The heart that Debbie has for Jesus in her daily life comes through in this great work. I believe you will be blessed and strengthened to love Jesus in a deeper way as you journey with Debbie through the Song of Solomon.

— ***Pastor Anthony Craver***
Upward Christian Fellowship

Intimacy with Father, Son, and Holy Spirit is the heart cry of every believer. When the barriers are removed, we have full access to the heart of God, His plans and purposes for us and for the world around us. The Greatest Romance is a gentle guide to that place of greater intimacy and encounter with Him. We encourage you to enter into this journey with great anticipation and expectation.

— Lee and Cindi Whitman
Executive Directors of Restoring the Foundations
www.restoringthefoundations.org
828-696-9075

As one of Debbie's closest friends for over twenty years, I can honestly say every word in this study comes from her greatest passion in life, to study the Word and pursue Jesus! Debbie has poured her heart and soul into this book for over ten years, and one of her greatest desires is to inspire others to hunger after the divine presence of God and have a deeper, more intimate relationship with Him.

— Teresa Weidner
www.cumberlandworshipcenter.org/
www.facebook.com/CumberlandWorshipCenter/

After pastoring churches for almost thirty years and editing over thirty-five study Bibles, I've pretty much heard everything. But one message never gets old: Jesus' undying love for me. That's why I love Debbie Welty's book. Verse by verse, Debbie uncovers Jesus' great love for us in the Song of Solomon. If you like to savor God's Word, this book is for you!

— Michael J. Klassen
Author, Speaker, and President of Illumify Media Global

the GREATEST ROMANCE

The Greatest Romance

Understand and Apply the Song of Solomon to Your Relationship with Jesus

DEBBIE WELTY

ILLUMIFY MEDIA GLOBAL
Littleton, Colorado

Copyright © 2020 by Debbie Welty

All rights reserved. No part of this book may be reproduced in any form or by any means—whether electronic, digital, mechanical, or otherwise—without permission in writing from the publisher, except by a reviewer, who may quote brief passages in a review.

Unless otherwise noted, all Scripture is taken from the King James Version. Public domain.

Scripture quotations marked NIV are from THE HOLY BIBLE, NEW INTERNATIONAL VERSION®, NIV®. Copyright © 1973, 1978, 1984, 2011 by Biblica, Inc.® Used by permission of Zondervan. All rights reserved worldwide. www.Zondervan.com. The "NIV" and "New International Version" are trademarks registered in the United States Patent and Trademark Office by Biblica, Inc.®

The views and opinions expressed in this book are those of the author and do not necessarily reflect the official policy or position of Illumify Media Global.

Published by
Illumify Media Global
www.IllumifyMedia.com
"Write. Publish. Market. SELL!"

Library of Congress Control Number: 2020913896

Paperback ISBN: 978-1-947360-60-0
eBook ISBN: 978-1-947360-61-7

Typeset by Art Innovations (http://artinnovations.in/)
Cover design by Debbie Lewis

Printed in the United States of America

Printed in the United States of America

The Greatest Romance
is dedicated to the Bridegroom.
Thank you for loving me.

CONTENTS

Introduction   xi

Song of Solomon 1
Week 1, Day 1:	The Kiss of Grace	1
Week 1, Day 2:	Accepted in the Beloved	8
Week 1, Day 3:	Beautiful and Valuable	13
Week 1, Day 4:	Exchanging Endearments	19
Week 1, Day 5:	Chapter Recap	26

Song of Solomon 2
Week 2, Day 1:	In His Shadow	30
Week 2, Day 2:	Do Not Disturb	38
Week 2, Day 3:	Come Away	43
Week 2, Day 4:	Possession	52
Week 2, Day 5:	Rise Up	56

Song of Solomon 3
Week 3, Day 1:	A LoneLy Soul on a Dark Night	60
Week 3, Day 2:	Desperation	65
Week 3, Day 3:	Intimacy Restored	72
Week 3, Day 4:	A Chariot Ride	77
Week 3, Day 5:	Jesus Really Does Loves Me	85

Song of Solomon 4
Week 4, Day 1:	Look at Yourself	88
Week 4, Day 2:	Brush Your Teeth	94
Week 4, Day 3:	Battle Ready yet Compassionate	99
Week 4, Day 4:	Spotless	104
Week 4, Day 5:	Fair and Fragrant	108

Song of Solomon 4 *(continued)*
Week 5, Day 1:	A Date with Jesus	112
Week 5, Day 2:	Passion	118
Week 5, Day 3:	Fragrant Worship	124
Week 5, Day 4:	Your Spirit	131
Week 5, Day 5:	Blow, Spirit . . . Blow	137

Song of Solomon 5
Week 6, Day 1:	An Intimate Dinner	144
Week 6, Day 2:	Awaken to His Call	150
Week 6, Day 3:	Watchmen That Destroy	160
Week 6, Day 4:	A Metaphorical Description of Jesus	164
Week 6, Day 5:	Awaken to His Love	175

Song of Solomon 6
Week 7, Day 1:	Truly Satisfied	181
Week 7, Day 2:	Spiritual Beauty	188
Week 7, Day 3:	Incomparable Beauty	196
Week 7, Day 4:	You're a Terrible Army	201
Week 7, Day 5:	Spiritual Warfare	208

Song of Solomon 7
Week 8, Day 1:	Spiritual Beauty	213
Week 8, Day 2:	Decked Out!	219
Week 8, Day 3:	A Sampling	224
Week 8, Day 4:	Open and Willing	229
Week 8, Day 5:	Desire	235

Song of Solomon 8
Week 8, Day 1:	Spiritual Intimacy	239
Week 9, Day 2:	Rest in His Embrace	243
Week 9, Day 3:	Out of the Wilderness	247
Week 9, Day 4:	Vows	251
Week 9, Day 5:	Intimacy	256

Song of Solomon 8 *(continued)*
Week 10, Day 1:	The Lost	259
Week 10, Day 2:	Favored	263
Week 10, Day 3:	Keeper of the Vineyard	266
Week 10, Day 4:	Longing for His Return	272
Week 10, Day 5:	The Mature	275

Conclusion: The Song of all Songs	280
Bibliography	281
About the Author	282

INTRODUCTION

While Song of Solomon is grouped with the poetic books of the Bible, there are several methods of interpretation to consider. Orthodox Christianity uses an allegorical approach to the book. Song of Solomon is a beautiful allegory of romance and intimacy, depicting the mutual love of Christ and the church.

There is also the typological method of interpretation, which focuses on the actual marriage of King Solomon and a non-Israeli princess (Henry). This foreshadows the union of Christ with the Gentiles and is very similar to an allegorical interpretation.

This unusual book is also interpreted using the literal method, which celebrates marriage and the love a husband and wife should enjoy (Bullock). Bible commentaries agree that deeper meaning than a virtuous marriage can be found in the book, both for Jews and Christians.

God entered into a covenant with Israel, which He, Himself, compared to a marriage covenant. In Isaiah 62:4–5; Jeremiah 3:1, and Hosea 2:16–19, God refers to Himself as the husband and to the Jews as His bride.

Under the new covenant, Jesus is referred to as the bridegroom and the church is referred to as the bride (Matthew 25:1; Romans 7:4; 2 Corinthians 11:2; Revelation 21:2–9).

In light of God's covenant with Israel, and of Christ returning as a bridegroom for His bride (the church), an allegorical interpretation is in keeping with the whole of scripture. *The Greatest Romance* will treat the poetic love song as an allegory portraying not only God's love for Israel but also and primarily, Christ's love for the church and that of the church for Him.

The chapters are full of symbolism, metaphors, and poetic imagery, but with determined research, Christ and the church can be found throughout. The intimacy that God desires to have with the church and even with individuals, the intimacy that was made available to us through Christ is found in this book. Due to the underlying sensual nature of the material, care will be taken to capture the truth that while we love the Lord with all our heart, soul, mind, and strength, the depth of that love is in the realm of the spirit.

Before we get into the study, I want to assure you that I have thoroughly completed the necessary research to root out cultural influences and original Hebraic word meanings, as well as consulted many commentaries and study guides on the material presented. I found it best to use the King James Version because *Strong's Concordance* and many of the commentaries are based on that text.

I believe it is very appropriate to personalize Song of Solomon and take it to heart as an individual. As we already noted, it can be interpreted in several ways:

- Solomon's marriage and love for his wife (wives).
- God's love for Israel, whom He referred to as His wife.
- Christ's love for the church, whom He referrers to as His soon to be bride.
- Christ's love for us as individuals. He died for each of us.

My friends, you are in for a real treat. Some of the truths from this beautiful book blew my mind. Just brace yourself for a deep and very personal revelation of Jesus' love. The symbols and metaphors will be explored fully in the following pages so that you can discover that the Savior loves you passionately and that He deeply longs for you to love Him passionately in return.

WEEK ONE

Song of Solomon 1:1–4

THE KISS OF GRACE

Are you ready to dive into this incredibly romantic book? Before we do, let's go over the format of this study. First, I will present each verse in the King James Version and then I will unlock the symbolism. After that, the verse will be presented again replacing the symbolism with words we can apply to our relationship with Jesus.

Immediately, within the first four verses of chapter 1, we have words that conjure up sexual images such as kiss, love, and chamber (which indicates the bedchamber). Like many people, you are probably wondering what this is doing in the Bible and what you're supposed to do with it. These verses are very intimate and personal because they are a picture of the salvation experience. The salvation experience is meant to be very intimate and personal. Take a moment to reflect on your own salvation experience and how deeply it touched you. Salvation is not merely a mental acknowledgment of the truth of the Gospel. A true salvation experience will touch a person's spirit, the very core of their being. That's why the text contains words of intimacy such as kiss, love, and bedchamber. I want us to look closely at each verse so that we can begin to grasp the depth of His love for us and so that we would yield more completely to His love.

VERSE 1:
"The song of songs, which is Solomon's."

The first phrase identifies the book as a song. It has also been identified as a poem, which is why I like to read it in stanzas. The author is King Solomon. He is known as the wise king and he declares that his song is "the song of songs." This means it is better than all other songs because it is symbolic of Christ's song of love to us. It's wise to celebrate the love of God and point others to it. Below you will see verse 1 in the original King James Version, with my interpretation of it on the right:

KJV	MY VERSION
"The song of songs, which is Solomon's."	"This love song is the best of all songs because it's Christ's song of love to me."

VERSE 2:
"Let him kiss me with the kisses of his mouth: for thy love is better than wine."

The stage has been set for romance and a theme of intimacy. The bride, addressing the bridegroom, asks for kisses. I had to do some serious studying and praying to unlock the meaning of the word "kiss." Using Scripture as my primary guide to symbolism, this kiss speaks of reconciliation and forgiveness. In the Old Testament, Esau kissed Jacob as a sign of forgiveness and reconciliation. In the New Testament, the father kissed the prodigal son, showing forgiveness and reconciliation. It is our responsibility to call out to Jesus for this kiss: for the salvation of our souls, for the forgiveness of our sins, and for grace, which will reconcile us to the Father. Psalm 2:12 tells us our responsibility is summed up in us kissing the Son. Grace, forgiveness, and salvation can be summed up in the Son kissing us.

The bride tells the bridegroom that His kiss of grace and reconciliation is love. She also says that His kiss is better than wine. Wine has a particular effect on us. It makes our hearts feel glad and light. It exhilarates and revives us. His love is more effective than wine in making our hearts glad and reviving our spirits. Based on those truths, here's my interpretation of verse 2:

KJV	MY VERSION
"Let him kiss me with the kisses of his mouth: for thy love is better than wine."	"Jesus, kiss me with the kiss of grace, forgiveness, and reconciliation, for Your love refreshes and revives me better than wine."

VERSE 3:
"Because of the savour of thy good ointments thy name is as ointment poured forth, therefore do the virgins love thee."

I found that the word *savour* is the key to unlocking the meaning of verse 3. The Hebrew definition of the word is "an odor, scent, or smell which is blown across the room." *Blown across* denotes wind. I thought about the Holy Spirit appearing as a wind in Acts 2. Much like the wind carries a fragrance found in the air, verse 3 is a picture of the Holy Spirit who carries the grace and love of God to us. The Holy Spirit is also found in the word *ointment*. Its Hebrew definition is "anointing oil." This savory anointing oil is poured forth like the Holy Spirit as described in Joel 2:28. Grace, forgiveness, reconciliation, and all that the name of Jesus makes available to us is poured upon us by the Holy Spirit. "Poured forth" points to a continual and generous outpouring. This outpouring of grace and goodness causes the virgins, those made pure in heart by His forgiveness and gift of righteousness, to love Him. Putting these thoughts together, here's my interpretation of verse 3:

KJV	MY VERSION
"Because of the saviour of thy good ointments, thy name is as ointment poured forth, therefore do the virgins love thee."	"Holy Spirit has carried Your fragrance of love and grace to me. Jesus, all that Your name makes available is being poured upon me by the Holy Spirit. It's no wonder the pure in heart, the forgiven, love You. I love You, Jesus."

VERSE 4:
"Draw me, we will run after thee: the king hath brought me into his chambers: we will be glad and rejoice in thee, we will remember thy love more than wine: the upright love thee."

"Draw me" shows that the bride desires closeness and intimacy of spirit. Jeremiah 31:3 and John 6:44 both show that our relationship with Jesus starts with Him drawing us. She has tasted His kiss of grace, been overwhelmed by His love, and smelt the fragrance of His anointing. All of this has caused her to desire a more intimate relationship with Him.

Her desire is strong enough to drive her to pursue Him. The bride starts with "draw me" and progresses to "we will run after thee." The *we* is representative of "me and mine, all in my house, all under my influence." Notice that her request to be drawn is immediately granted as the next phrase reads, "the king brought me into his chambers." Dear one, Jesus is eagerly waiting for us to pursue intimacy with Him.

Let's identify the king in this passage. To some, it is a reference to Christ, the King of kings; while to others, it is a reference to King Solomon. Perhaps it is helpful to realize that King Solomon was a type or shadow of Christ. Notice the commonalities. They were both kings in the succession of King David. King Solomon was the builder and founder of the temple. Christ was the founder of the New Testament Church. Solomon excelled in wisdom and wealth. In Christ is hidden all the treasures of wisdom and knowledge.

"The king hath brought me into His chambers" is indicative of the sexual intimacy that takes place in the bedroom of a husband and wife. Keep in mind that our intimacy with Christ is spiritual, not sexual. Notice, however, that after entering into the chambers, the bride refers to herself as *we*. This indicates not only the oneness, which is a result of the consummation of marriage, but also denotes conception to the multiplying of those that rejoice in Him. Our spiritual intimacy with Christ will cause us to bring forth fruit, multiplying His followers. It will also bring us to a place of oneness with Him.

The next two phrases in verse 4 are repetitive from verses 2 and 3. The bride is declaring, again, that His love, which was experienced in the bedchamber, is better than wine. His love makes her heart light and glad. That's why the pure in heart (those forgiven and made righteous by Him) love Him. Here is my translation of verse 4.

KJV	MY VERSION
"Draw me, we will run after thee: The king hath brought me into his chambers: we will be glad and rejoice in thee, we will remember thy love more than wine: the upright love thee."	"Pull me toward yourself, Jesus, I want to experience more of Your love. I will bring those I influence with me into Your arms of love. Oh! King Jesus has brought me into His bed-chamber. My companions and I are so light and happy. We are overjoyed with pleasure in You, Jesus. Your love revives and refreshes us better than wine. You have made me righteous and I love You, Jesus."

We have dissected all the symbolism in the first four verses, replacing it with words we can understand and apply to our relationship with Jesus. Starting with verse 1, progressing to verse 2 and so on, please go back through today's study and reread my translation for each verse. As you read it, be drawn into intimacy with Him.

Reflections

Have you received the kiss of grace? If so, write a brief description of your salvation experience. If not, maybe you want to use this space to ask Him for that kiss.

_____

_____

According to verse 3, what part does the Holy Spirit play in the salvation experience?

___

Response

Spend some time with the One whose love is better than wine, then journal about your time with Him.

___

WEEK ONE

Song of Solomon 1:5–7

ACCEPTED IN THE BELOVED

Starting at verse 5 and continuing through verse 7, the mood changes drastically from one of romance to feelings of inferiority. Sadly, this is quite common in our Christian experience. Satan opposes our intimacy with Jesus. He brings things to our memory that cause us to feel unworthy of our Savior's love, ultimately causing us to withdraw from Christ. Notice the discouragement and despair in the bride's voice as she now addresses the church as signified by "daughters of Jerusalem."

VERSE 5:
*"I am black, but comely, O ye daughters of Jerusalem,
as the tents of Kedar, as the curtains of Solomon."*

The bride has become introspective. She perceives herself as black, or unworthy of all that Christ has done for her, but at the same time, she realizes that what He has done has made her comely. She is conflicted. Have you ever been conflicted? I sure have. Introspection will usually lead to conflicting feelings and confusion. Be sure it's from the enemy.

The tents and curtains refer to items of that era that were literally stained black in color. Here is my interpretation of verse 5:

KJV	MY VERSION
"I am black, but comely, O ye daughters of Jerusalem, as the tents of Kedar, as the curtains of Solomon."	"Wait, how can I be righteous? I am stained. I assure you, my friends, I am not righteous, not worthy of love."

VERSE 6:
"Look not upon me, because I am black, because the sun hath looked upon me: my mother's children were angry with me; they made me the keeper of the vineyards; but mine own vineyard have I not kept."

In verse 6, she gives reasons for her condition of unworthiness. The sun signifies exposure to the harsh elements in the world, elements that beat us down. These feelings of unworthiness are also due to persecution as indicated by the reference to her abusive siblings. There is also the matter of her own sin, her own vineyard, which she did not keep.

These feelings of rejection, inadequacy, or unworthiness will keep us from pursuing intimacy with Christ. Maybe you can relate to these types of feelings. Whether they stem from guilt over personal sin or from being treated unkindly (devalued and abused) by others, these feelings will limit your ability to enter into intimacy with Christ and even with other people. It is a worthless, hopeless, lonely feeling and is quite common among Christians. It is something we must overcome so that we can move into intimacy with Christ. Verse 6 in my own words:

KJV	MY VERSION
"Look not upon me, because I am black, because the sun hath looked upon me: my mother's children were angry with me; they made me the keeper of the vineyards; but mine own vineyard have I not kept."	"Do not look at me! I cannot possibly be worthy of love. The world has treated me unkindly. My own family has abused and rejected me. And I have sinned, all on my own. I am a sinner. I am not righteous. I am stained."

VERSE 7:

"Tell me, O thou whom my soul loveth, where thou feedest, where thou makest thy flock to rest at noon: for why should I be as one that turneth aside by the flocks of thy companions?"

Her condition causes her to look for rest from the struggle of unworthiness. I love how verse 7 is a picture of Psalm 23, where Christ is the shepherd who feeds His flock and gives them rest. She asks herself and Him why she should look for relief elsewhere. In the past, His love caused her heart to be light and glad. This is what she is seeking again.

Thank the Lord that we can find relief from these negative feelings about ourselves. We find relief and acceptance in His love. Ephesians 1:6 says: "To the praise of the glory of His grace, in which He has made us accepted in the beloved." We should never turn elsewhere for acceptance and love. My rendition of verse 7:

KJV	MY VERSION
"Tell me, O thou whom my soul loveth, where thou feedest, where thou makest thy flock to rest at noon: for why should I be as one that turneth aside by the flocks of thy companions?"	"Tell me, Jesus, whom I love with all my soul, where can I find rest from these feelings of unworthiness, inadequacy, and rejection? Where do You feed, and nurture Your redeemed, those You ransomed for Yourself? I am Yours. Why should I look elsewhere for acceptance and rest?"

Praise God, we are accepted in Christ! Go back now and read the translated verses altogether. In tomorrow's lesson, we will find that He answers her very quickly and puts the issue of our value to rest.

Reflections

Describe any feelings of unworthiness or inferiority that you struggle with. What do you think they are rooted in?

_____

_____

_____

To what extent have you experienced emotional or physical abuse?

_____

_____

_____

Can you believe that it is Satan who magnifies the feelings of unworthiness or inferiority in your mind? Why would he do that?

_____

_____

_____

Response

Pour your heart out to Jesus. Tell Him everything regarding these issues. His response to you will unfold tomorrow as we look at verses 8–11.

_____

_____

_____

_____

WEEK ONE

Song of Solomon 1:8–11

BEAUTIFUL AND VALUABLE

*I*n verses 5–7, the bride was speaking to Jesus. She asked where she could find relief from feelings of unworthiness, inadequacy, and shame. Starting with verse 8, Christ begins to speak to her. I love that He answers her so quickly. These verses (8–11) are among my favorite as they express His feelings for us. My interpretations of these verses will be in italics to signify that Christ is speaking.

VERSE 8:
"If thou know not, O thou fairest among women, go thy way forth by the footsteps of the flock, and feed thy kids beside the shepherds' tents."

First, He addresses her assessment of herself as black. He calls her "fair," which is the opposite of black. The Hebrew root word for *fair* means "bright and beautiful." This is how He sees her: not stained with sin, not unrighteous; but righteous, clean, and bright. Beautiful! He welcomes her to find rest from unworthiness in His flock. The phrase "feed thy kids" shows that Christ wants to address these feelings in her generations past and future. I love that for my children and myself. Here's my interpretation:

KJV	MY VERSION
"If thou know not, O thou fairest among women, go thy way forth by the footsteps of the flock, and feed thy kids beside the shepherds' tents."	"You are not stained! Don't you know that you are bright and beautiful? You are radiant. Come unto Me. I will be as a shepherd to you. I will lead, feed and protect you. Bring your children too. Let them feed on Me, on My love and goodness."

VERSE 9:
"I have compared thee, O my love, to a company of horses in Pharaoh's chariots."

In verse 9, Christ compares His love (love is a noun, affectionately referring to me, to you, and the church) to a company of Pharaoh's horses. So, just stop for a second and laugh that Jesus compares you to a horse. That's wild! He is still addressing her unworthiness, showing her instead that she is valuable. Horses, especially Pharaoh's, indicated wealth and power. Pharaoh's horses were well bred, housed, fed, trained, and groomed. That's how valuable you are. He intends to take care of you, train (teach) you, and groom you for His service. You are valuable to Him. You make Him wealthy! Take a moment and make these declarations over yourself:

I am valuable to Him! I make Him wealthy!

That is overwhelming, but it's how He sees us. Enjoy my rendition of verse 9:

KJV	MY VERSION
"I have compared thee, O my love, to a company of horses in Pharaoh's chariots."	"You are so valuable to Me, O My love. Your value can be compared to a whole company of the best horses, The king's horses that pull his chariot. These are the most beautiful and strongest horses anywhere. They are housed, fed, and groomed royally to reflect the king's riches."

VERSE 10:

"Thy cheeks are comely with rows of jewels, thy neck with chains of gold."

Verse 10 speaks of jewels and chains of gold on the bride. Compare this to Isaiah 61:10, which shows this is proper adornment for a bride. This is how He sees her, spiritually adorned as His bride and worthy to be that bride. *Cheeks* indicate the soft part of the face. To me, the word *soft* speaks of a tender, trusting, and innocent spirit. *Neck* means the back of the neck (Strong's). I had to give some prayer and thought concerning what the back of the neck could mean. I believe it indicates humility because you only see the back of the neck when someone bows their head or body forward. For your comparison, my interpretation of verse 10 is on the right, with the King James Version on the left:

KJV	MY VERSION
"Thy cheeks are comely with rows of jewels, thy neck with chains of gold."	*"Your soft face, O My love, it is beautifully adorned with valuable jewels of tenderness, trust, innocence, and grace. You carry yourself humbly, which is of great value."*

VERSE 11:
"We will make thee borders of gold with studs of silver."

We refers to the trinity. Anything lacking in her will be supplied by Christ, His Father, and the Holy Spirit. From border to border, she will be spiritually perfect in beauty and value. Take a few minutes and read Isaiah 61:1–3 and realize that He wants to bring beauty, joy, and praise to every place in your life where you feel black, worthless, or inferior. You are a work in progress. He sees the finished product and declares your value and beauty! My presentation of verse 11:

KJV	MY VERSION
"We will make thee borders of gold with studs of silver."	*"Father, Holy Spirit and I will make all your borders as valuable as gold and silver."*

As we go forward with this study, please note that Jesus words will be italics. Now go back and reread just the translated verses, and please know that Jesus is declaring them over you. I hope these truths ministered to you on a very deep level.

Reflections

To what extent do you believe that you are valuable?

_____

_____

_____

To what extent do you believe that you are beautiful?

_____

_____

_____

What generational issues do you deal with?

_____

_____

_____

Response

Spend some time with Him. Thank Him for the kind words that He has spoken over you. Let Him minister to the wounded places in your life. Let Him bring healing and wholeness. Record your experience with Him here:

_____

_____

_____

_____

_____

_____

WEEK ONE

Song of Solomon 1:12–17

EXCHANGING ENDEARMENTS

These verses are touching endearments exchanged between the bride and the bridegroom. We will unlock all the symbolism so that the passage becomes applicable.

VERSE 12:
"While the king sitteth at his table,
my spikenard sendeth forth the smell thereof."

The king (Christ) is seated at His table where the bride's fragrance is evident, indicating that she is there with Him. She declares, "My spikenard sends forth the smell thereof." This speaks of worship—extremely intimate worship. Psalms 23:5 refers to a table that the Lord has prepared for us. 1 Corinthians 11:23–26 records the institution of the Lord's Table by Christ, where we are told to worshipfully remember His broken body and shed blood. Refresh your memory of John 12:1–3, where a house was filled with odor when Mary poured costly perfume, the exact kind mentioned in Song of Solomon, on the feet of Jesus as He was seated at a table for the Passover meal. Also, consider Luke 7:36–48, where a sinful woman broke an alabaster box containing fragrant ointment and poured it on Jesus' feet. She washed His feet, dried them with her hair, and kissed them with her mouth. Hair symbolizes a woman's glory. By absorbing oil with it and touching His feet with it, she traded her glory for His, realizing that she had none without Him. The alabaster box symbolizes the heart breaking forth in worship. Our worship is sweet incense to Him. Oh, how I love to worship Him! I hope you do too. In my interpretation of verse 12, the bride is speaking:

KJV	MY VERSION
"While the king sitteth at his table, my spikenard sendeth forth the smell thereof."	"As the King sits at His table, my extravagant worship becomes a fragrance in the air."

VERSE 13:

"A bundle of myrrh is my well-beloved unto me; he shall lie all night betwixt my breasts."

In verse 13, the bride calls Christ a bundle of myrrh, meaning a sweet smell that drips out slowly. This myrrh is the same oil in Psalms 23:5, where at that table in the presence of my enemy, the shepherd anoints my head with oil. This touches me. My worship releases a fragrance that pleases Him (verse 12), and He responds by releasing an anointing on my head. I hope you're overwhelmed by that truth. The bride was certainly overwhelmed with this anointing from Christ; so overwhelmed that she declares He will lie between her breasts all night. This beautiful picture of intimacy is simply Christ residing within our heart, which is located between the breasts. I interpret verse 13 like this:

KJV	MY VERSION
"A bundle of myrrh is my well-beloved unto me; he shall lie all night betwixt my breasts."	"And my Beloved's fragrance is also a sweet smell, it is an oil which drips out continually and slowly upon me. He will rest upon and in my heart all night."

VERSE 14:
"My beloved is unto me as a cluster of camphire in the vineyards of Engedi."

The bride calls Christ her beloved and compares Him to camphire. Figuratively, camphire represents a redemption, a ransom, or a sum of money. This is Christ, our Redeemer. He paid a great price for our salvation. The "vineyards of Engedi" are the source of the camphire. The source of our redemption is Father God. Engedi means "all-seeing eye from which life springs forth" (Henry). How cool is that! My interpretation of verse 14:

KJV	MY VERSION
"My beloved is unto me as a cluster of camphire in the vineyards of Engedi."	"He is my Beloved, my Redeemer, sent from God, the creator of all life who sees all things."

VERSE 15:
"Behold, thou art fair, my love; behold, thou art fair; thou hast doves' eyes."

Now Christ is addressing the bride. He is addressing me. He is addressing you. *Behold* signifies that He looks at her and sees her, once again, as "fair." *Behold* also indicates that this is how He wants her to see herself. He states this twice, indicating it's the truth. He says that she has dove's eyes. The dove is a symbol for the Holy Spirit as shown in Matthew 3:16. He is saying that she has eyes enlightened and guided by the Holy Spirit. Here is my presentation of verse 15:

KJV	MY VERSION
"Behold, thou art fair, my love; behold, thou art fair; thou hast doves' eyes."	*"Look at yourself, you are bright and beautiful, O My love, look, really look at yourself. You are bright and beautiful. You now have eyes that see in the realm of the spirit. Look and see that you are bright, radiant, and beautiful."*

VERSE 16:
"Behold, thou art fair, my beloved, yea, pleasant: also our bed is green."

Since the bride referred to Christ as "my beloved" in verse 14, it follows that this is her speaking in verse 16. She is responding to His gentle prompt to look at herself in the realm of the spirit (with her dove's eyes). After beholding her spiritual appearance and seeing that it truly is beautiful, she realizes that it is merely a reflection of His beauty and she expresses that to Him.

"Our bed is green" refers to the fruit of marriage, which is multiplication. Here's my interpretation of what she could now see in the realm of the spirit:

KJV	MY VERSION
"Behold, thou art fair, my beloved, yea, pleasant: also our bed is green."	"I am looking. I see that You are bright and beautiful, my beloved Jesus. My brightness and beauty are merely a reflection of Yours. Yes, You are very pleasant to behold. I also see that our intimacy bears fruit."

VERSE 17:

"The beams of our house are cedar, and our rafters of fir."

She continues to adore Him (verse 17), appreciating the stability of their relationship. Cedar and fir are both durable, sweet-smelling woods that do not rot easily or quickly like other woods (Henry). She is rejoicing in her eternal security in His love. My rendition of verse 17 explains this:

KJV	MY VERSION
"The beams of our house are cedar, and our rafters of fir."	"I see that this relationship is secure and will last for eternity."

This is so romantic. That's how your relationship with Jesus is meant to be. He loves you completely and hopes you will respond to His love with worship and adoration. He also hopes that you will believe Him when He speaks words of endearment over you. Read through the translated verses of today's study and remember that Jesus' words are in italics.

As we finish the first chapter, I hope your heart is full and overwhelmed by His love for you. I hope His love has refreshed you like wine. I pray that you have stepped into a deeper level of intimacy with the lover of your soul.

Reflections

Describe a time of worship when you felt as though He was right there with you.

_____

_____

_____

To what extent does worship change your perspective? Why do you think that is?

_____

_____

_____

Response

Worship Him, then let Him love on you. Try to hear Him speaking endearments over you. Ask Him for eyes like a dove's (eyes that see in the realm of the spirit). Describe what you see. Record your experience with Him here.

_____

_____

_____

_____

_____

_____

WEEK ONE

Song of Solomon 1

CHAPTER RECAP

It's easy to recognize the salvation experience portrayed with the kiss of grace. The chapter also contains the message of acceptance. Many times, those who experience salvation stop there in their spiritual journey. They do not enter into intimacy with Jesus because of feelings of unworthiness. They are afraid to press for His love beyond salvation. Rejection is a very real fear. Ephesians 1:6 says: "To the praise of the glory of His grace, in which He has made us accepted in the beloved." Accepted means we are accepted, worthy, valuable, lovable, and loved. His kiss of grace makes us beautiful and desirable. He truly wants a deep intimate relationship with us.

Based on the symbolism that we uncovered throughout the chapter, allow me the liberty to present the following rendition of chapter 1 in terms that we can understand and relate to. Please don't just read the words. Speak them to Jesus. Be drawn into intimacy with Him. Let Him touch and bless your heart. Enjoy the wine as He kisses you with the kiss of grace. His words are in italics for easy flow. Receive the words He speaks over you.

"This love song is the best of all songs
because it's Christ's song of love to me.
Jesus, kiss me with the kiss of grace,
forgiveness, and reconciliation,
for Your love refreshes and revives me better than wine.
Holy Spirit has carried Your fragrance of love and grace to me.
Jesus, all that Your name makes available is being poured
upon me by Holy Spirit.
It's no wonder the pure in heart, the forgiven, love You.
I love You, Jesus.
Pull me toward Yourself, Jesus,
I want to experience more of Your love.
I will bring those I influence with me into Your arms of love.
Oh! King Jesus has brought me into His bed-chamber.
My companions and I are so light and happy.
We are overjoyed with pleasure in You, Jesus.
Your love revives and refreshes us better than wine.
You have made me righteous and I love You, Jesus.
Wait, how can I be righteous? I am stained.
I assure you, my friends,
I am not righteous, not worthy of love.
Do not look at me! I cannot possibly be worthy of love.
The world has treated me unkindly.
My own family has abused and rejected me.
And I have sinned, all on my own. I am a sinner.
I am not righteous. I am stained.
Tell me, Jesus, whom I love with all my soul,
Where can I find rest from these feelings
of unworthiness, inadequacy, and rejection?
Where do You feed, and nurture Your redeemed,
those You ransomed for Yourself?

I am Yours.
Why should I look elsewhere for acceptance and rest?
You are not stained!
Don't you know that you are bright and beautiful?
You are radiant.
Come unto Me. I will be as a shepherd to you.
I will lead, feed and protect you.
Bring your children too.
Let them feed on Me, on My love and goodness.
You are so valuable to Me, O My love.
Your value can be compared to a whole company of the best horses,
The king's horses that pull his chariot.
These are the most beautiful and strongest horses anywhere.
They are housed, fed, and groomed royally
to reflect the king's riches.
Your soft face, O My love,
It is beautifully adorned with valuable jewels
of tenderness, trust, innocence, and grace.
You carry yourself humbly, which is of great value.
Father, Holy Spirit and I will make all your borders
as valuable as gold and silver.
As the King sits at His table,
My extravagant worship becomes a fragrance in the air.
And my Beloved's fragrance is also a sweet smell,
It is an oil that drips out continually and slowly upon me.
He will rest upon and in my heart all night.
He is my Beloved, my Redeemer,
sent from God, the Creator of all life who sees all things.
Look at yourself; you are bright and beautiful,
O My love, look, really look at yourself.
You are bright and beautiful.
You now have eyes that see in the realm of the spirit.

Look and see that you are bright, radiant, and beautiful.
I am looking.
I see that You are bright and beautiful, my beloved Jesus.
My brightness and beauty are merely a reflection of Yours.
Yes, You are very pleasant to behold.
I also see that our intimacy bears fruit.
I see that this relationship is secure and will last for eternity."

Reflection and Response

If you are doing this as a group Bible study, use day five as the day you come together. Go over the refection questions from each day together. Share, encourage, and pray for one another.

_____

_____

_____

If you are doing this study on your own, review the reflection and response sections from each day. Worship Him and ask Him to do a deeper work. Ask Him to add another layer of truth and beauty to your heart. Record your experience with Him here.

_____

_____

_____

WEEK TWO

Song of Solomon 2:1–4

IN HIS SHADOW

Chapter 2, like chapter 1, is very sensual. In it, the Lord is communicating the depth of His love, affection, and passion for us in terms that we can understand. We should thoughtfully apply the message of His love to our souls in the realm of the spirit.

Christ is speaking in verse 1, comparing Himself to earthly things so that we can identify with what He is trying to tell us.

VERSE 1:
"I am the rose of Sharon, and the lily of the valleys."

He is much more than any earthly thing. He is the Son of the Highest, yet He calls Himself the rose of Sharon and the lily of the valleys. Why does He refer to Himself as two flowers? He does this to show that He is present in this world just as the flowers are. He is showing that He is accessible to us just like flowers are tangible. He is showing us that He is beautiful, like flowers. He is showing us that He has a sweet fragrance, like flowers. And lastly, He shows us that we should adorn ourselves with His beauty and fragrance just as we adorn ourselves with flowers.

Let's look closer at each flower mentioned. Sharon was a place where roses grew in abundance and were easily accessible (Henry). The phrase "rose of Sharon" signifies that Christ's grace, comfort, and salvation are available in abundance. He is not in some private garden that is hard to find. His grace is not difficult to obtain. His salvation, His love, and His comfort are accessible to all.

There is quite a bit of symbolism associated with lilies. They are white, which denotes purity. Jesus is pure. He never sinned (2 Corinthians 5:21). Lilies release a strong, sweet odor. I have heard of people smelling a sweet fragrance while in the presence of the Lord. The "lily of the valleys" refers to the low places. This is a picture of Christ's humility in that He, the Son of God, humbled Himself and died for us. The lily also speaks of regeneration as it seemly comes back to life after the harsh winter months where it was perceived as dead. This speaks of Christ's resurrection and of eternal life for us. This is what Christ is saying to us in verse 1:

KJV	MY VERSION
"I am the rose of Sharon, and the lily of the valleys."	"I am the desired, beautiful, fragrant One. My grace, mercy, and love are accessible and available to all. I am pure, humble, and I am Life."

VERSE 2:
"As the lily among thorns, so is my love among the daughters."

He calls us lilies. He is saying that we are like Him. We are pure because of Him. We have taken on His fragrance, and we release it to the world around us. We, too, are called to a humble life of sacrifice. We, too, will live forever.

Check out Matthew 6:28–29 where Jesus compares and even preferers the beauty of the lilies above the apparel of King Solomon with all its glory. Our apparel in the spiritual realm has greater glory than rich King Solomon's. Our spiritual apparel is white and pure. That's a picture of the robe of righteousness mentioned in Isaiah 61:10. We are pure, fragrant, beautiful, and desirable, just like our Savior.

We are as lilies among thorns. Thorns symbolize the wicked, or those who are without Christ. Their spiritual apparel is filthy. They have no purity and have no sweet fragrance. Thorns are hurtful, undesirable, and often noxious. They choke good seeds and hinder good fruit (Matthew 13:7). Their end is to be burned (Matthew 13:30).

Just like lilies grow among thorns, we (like Christ was) are exposed to hardship and troubles in this world. We must never act like thorns by becoming noxious or hurtful. In verse 2, Christ tells us:

KJV	**MY VERSION**
"As the lily among thorns, so is my love among the daughters."	*"You, My love, are alive, desired, beautiful, fragrant, valuable, and pure in Me. You dwell among filthy, wicked, hurtful, noxious lost ones. You dwell among hardship and danger; and yet you thrive."*

VERSE 3:
"As the apple tree among the trees of the wood, so is my beloved among the sons. I sat down under his shadow with great delight, and his fruit was sweet to my taste."

The bride is speaking here. She expresses her preference for Christ over the other sons of God. This refers to both men and angels. Intimacy with Christ will satisfy you on an emotional and spiritual level. Intimacy with Christ will enhance your marriage. You will stop looking to your spouse to meet emotional and spiritual needs that only Christ can meet.

And for as angels, many people worship angels. This is very dangerous, as only a fallen angel would allow you to worship him.

She likens Christ to an apple tree when compared to other trees of the woods. In the Bible, trees often represent men (Mark 8:24). She is comparing Jesus to all other men. The apple tree provides shade and fruit. She experienced great comfort as she sat in His cool shadow, protected from the scorching heat. She describes sitting in His shadow as a delight. I am reminded of Psalm 91 where we dwell under the shadow of the Almighty. Imagine the protection and absolute comfort of being cooled, refreshed, and strengthened in His shadow, as well as nourished by the fruit of this apple tree. Partaking of Christ nourishes and satisfies our souls like nothing else can.

Think for a moment about the cross. It was made from a tree. We need to sit down in its shadow. The shadow of the cross saves us from the heat and fire of hell. It offers the fruit of righteousness and the fruit of the spirit. It offers us life. She "sat down" to rest.

We can sit down in His shadow, at His feet, with delight. We can put our entire confidence in the protection and provision of our Savior. We have no work to do. We do not have to earn this rest, nor can we. It has all been done for us at the cross. Only spiritual rest brings real peace. When spiritual peace is attained, emotional and mental rest soon follow. Then we can relax physically and receive rest for our bodies.

She declares that the "fruit was sweet." It was refreshing. Fruit is the provision of all that the covenant provides. Fruit includes all the promises of God. It includes all that Christ's blood secured for us. "Taste and see that the Lord is good" (Psalm 34:8). When you eat something good, you often want more. My interpretation of verse 3 is her response to Him.

KJV	MY VERSION
"As the apple tree among the trees of the wood, so is my beloved among the sons. I sat down under his shadow with great delight, and his fruit was sweet to my taste."	"There is no one else like my Beloved. His covering protects me and keeps me safe. I rest in the shadow of His cross. I am secure in His saving grace. I love all that He offers me. It's a banquet of life, beauty, grace, mercy, purity, love, and salvation."

I believe the fruit was so delightful to her that she was ready to experience more and this prompted His next move.

VERSE 4:
"He brought me to the banqueting house, and his banner over me was love."

He "brought me" or took me by the hand and guided me. He helped me over obstacles, over my discouragements, over my unworthiness, over my shame, and over my fears. He gently leads us into deeper things. We find a progression here. He sees her under the shadow, delighting in His protection from the heat, resting in His provision of salvation, joy, and peace, enjoying His fruit and abundant blessings. This mirrors basic salvation. He sees her there. He allows her to sit there, but He doesn't leave her there. This progression is an invitation to deeper intimacy. The banquet represents a place of spiritual fullness and spiritual feasting, complete with wine. "He brought me to the house of wine" is the literal Hebrew translation of the phrase "He brought me to the banqueting house." All of this started at the fruit of the tree (cross), which is salvation;

it progressed to the fruit of the vine (wine), which is the Holy Spirit's infilling. Remember that wine makes the heart glad!

I encourage every reader to be hungry for the infilling of the Spirit. Pursue and seek the Baptism of the Holy Spirit as describes in Acts 2:4,17. Holy Spirit enhances your relationship with Jesus. Just like a person can become addicted to wine, the Holy Spirit becomes almost like that addiction. It's an addiction to His presence.

Let's talk about the banner of His love. We see a lot of banners in churches today. Often, they portray the beauty and majesty of God. They are very pretty but they are much more than that. A banner over someone declares their identity. For example, the United States flag declares that this is the USA. The flag symbolizes our freedom and rights as US citizens. The US flag is a military statement. It's a warning to our enemy! The banner of Christ's love over us identifies us as His. We belong to him. His banner of love over us is real in the realm of the spirit. By it, the Lord declares to our enemy, "Hands off! This one is mine." The banner protects our freedom and rights as a child of God. The bride in Song of Solomon was amazed and declared that she was allowed into this intimate place of communion with God because of the banner of Christ's love over her head.

Think about Christ's love for us. His love is strong and powerful in our lives. It is also powerful against our enemy. His love is unconditional and unchanging. Yet, His love changes us! That's powerful love. Paul prayed that we would be rooted and grounded in it (Ephesians 3:16–19).

This verse is packed with significance, but let's focus on this: we can and should become addicted to His love. As my rendition of verse 4 shows, she is delighted in Him.

KJV	MY VERSION
"He brought me to the banqueting house, and his banner over me was love."	"He leads and helps me over every obstacle into deeper intimacy with Himself, Into the fullness of His love, which is better than wine. My heart is made glad and light. His love covers me, protects me and secures victory for me."

I love the first 4 verses of chapter 2. Reread just the translated verses. This is a conversation between Christ and His bride, each one expressing their love for the other. His words are differentiated with italics. I hope you have conversations with Jesus, expressing your love and appreciation to Him. When you do, don't forget to listen for His response.

Reflections

In your own words, what does "the rose of Sharon" mean for you?

_____

_____

_____

In your own words, what does Christ being "the lily of the valleys" mean for you?

_____

_____

_____

Response

Spend some time loving on Him and let Him love on you. Respond to His invitation to eat at His banqueting table. Record your encounter with Him. Recording these encounters is an action that solidifies the reality of the encounter.

_____

_____

_____

_____

_____

_____

WEEK TWO

Song of Solomon 2:5–7

DO NOT DISTURB

Day one ended with the bride expressing her delight in the banquet of His love. Having thoroughly enjoyed the intimacy they shared, she now expresses her desire for even more of His love.

VERSE 5:
"Stay me with flagons, comfort me with apples, for I am sick of love."

Flagons comes from a root word that refers to pressing down on something to form a sure foundation. *Flagons* also refers to flowers and fruits that were pressed into ointments for their fragrance. She is asking that through pressing they become one and that He becomes the foundation or rock upon which her life is built. This pressing is a vivid picture of sexual intimacy where a couple become one. Wow!

She asks to be comforted with apples. Apples represent fruit, as in the fruit of the Spirit. She desires more love, joy, peace, patience, gentleness, goodness, faith, meekness, and self-control. These attributes of her lover bring her much comfort and she wants to be like Him. She wants this fruit in her life.

She declares her love for Him by saying, "I am sick of love," which means she is overcome and overpowered by His love. She expresses her love for Him by asking for more. Let's stop for a moment and do that. Express your love to Jesus. Ask Him for more. Pray this with me: *Jesus, press in on me with Your love, become the foundation of my life, comfort me with Your goodness, Your love, Your grace, Your fragrance. Press in on me. Overwhelm and overpower me until we are truly one. I am overcome with love and desire for You. Amen.*

Are we being greedy or maybe needy asking Jesus for more? No, we are yielding, surrendering to His desire to love us. He longs for those He loves to love Him back. She loves Him and welcomes more of His love. Below is my interpretation of verse 5:

KJV	MY VERSION
"Stay me with flagons, comfort me with apples: for I am sick of love."	"Oh Jesus, press down on me until we are one, And continue pressing until You have become the foundation of my life. Comfort me with grace and mercy. For I am all together overcome by Your love."

VERSE 6:
"His left hand is under my head, and his right hand doth embrace me."

Sometimes when you are overcome with His love, His glory, and weightiness, you faint or fall under the weight of it. This is what happened.

"I am sick of love. I'm being overcome by it. I am falling under its power." Scripture gives several examples of saints being overcome by His love and falling under the weight of it (2 Chronicles 5:14, 1 Kings 8:11, Daniel 10:8, Revelation 1:17). Today this experience is often referred to as "falling out in the Spirit." In verse 6, the bridegroom catches her with His hand as she is falling under the weight and glory of His love. He supports her, holds her, and embraces her. This paints a very intimate picture. Verses 5 and 6 both contain pictures of sexual intimacy, which demonstrate to us the level of spiritual intimacy the Lord wants with us. My interpretation of verse 6 is on the right:

KJV	MY VERSION
"His left hand is under my head, and his right hand doth embrace me."	"He is holding me now for I have fallen under the power and glory of His love. His left hand is under my head, and His right hand embraces me."

VERSE 7:
"I charge you, O ye daughters of Jerusalem, by the roes, and by the hinds of the field, that ye stir not up, nor awake my love, till he please."

Thoroughly enjoying the intimacy and the closeness of her lover, she takes great care that her communion with Him is not interrupted. She charges herself and all about her to be still. She is commanding, "Do not disturb this intimacy!"

Roes and hinds are members of the deer family. They are disturbed easily and run away at the slightest movement. She commands her mind to be still, her thoughts to be captivated, stayed on Him and Him alone!

Those intimate times do eventually come to an end. We arise from those times refreshed, renewed, healed, sensing His love on a deeper level, and wanting more. However, it is necessary to get back into the routines and responsibilities of life where we yearn for another intimate time with Him. "My soul longs for, faints for the courts of my God" (Psalm 84:2). He longs for more intimacy with you too. My interpretation of verse 7 looks like this:

KJV	MY VERSION
"I charge you, O ye daughters of Jerusalem, by the roes, and by the hinds of the field, that ye stir not up, nor awake my love, till he please."	"I command my heart, my mind, even my friends to be still. Do not disturb my Beloved! Be still for He is easily disturbed and will flee away from our intimate time."

Such profound intimacy is portrayed in verses 5–7. The pressing in verse 5, the embrace in verse 6, and the charge for stillness in verse 7 are all a picture of sexual intimacy between a man and his wife. They are a picture of the spiritual intimacy that Jesus longs for with you. Keep that in mind as you go back and reread the translated verses.

Reflections

How do you feel about the level of spiritual intimacy described in Solomon 2:5–7?

_____

_____

_____

What level of intimacy do you enjoy with Jesus? To what degree do you desire a deeper level?

_____

_____

_____

Response

Express your love to Him. Stir up desire for Him. Ask Him for more; ask for a deeper revelation of His love. Record your encounter with Him.

_____

_____

_____

WEEK TWO

Song of Solomon 2:8–15

COME AWAY

That wonderful time of intimacy, the one covered in verses 5–7, which included pressing and embracing, must have been interrupted. Life does have a way of moving on. Jesus understands this. As long as we are open to intimacy, He always comes back. Let's start breaking down what verses 8–15 mean by uncovering all the symbolism.

VERSES 8–9:
"The voice of my beloved! Behold, he cometh leaping upon the mountains, skipping upon the hills. My beloved is like a roe or a young hart."

She heard His voice, and she recognized it immediately. "My sheep know My voice" (John 10:4). She exclaimed, "It's His voice, my Beloved!" She expressed such joy and anticipation when she realized He was coming close again.

He came leaping over mountains and skipping over hills like a roe or a young hart. The word *roe* signifies something of beauty and splendor, something very prominent that comes forth with the boldness and fury of an army. *Hart* refers to the strength of the animal. Just imagine the physical, political, spiritual, and authoritative strength of our Savior. Christ is like the roe or the hart in that He quickly, easily, and skillfully overcomes everything that stands between Himself and us. Every discouragement, every opposition—His strength and authority will break through it for us. He leaps with strength and authority over every obstacle between us, big or small. She saw Him in the very act of breaking through on her behalf. She couldn't help but be excited and proclaim my interpretation of verses 8 and 9:

KJV	MY VERSION
"The voice of my beloved! Behold, he cometh leaping upon the mountains, skipping upon the hills. My beloved is like a roe or a young hart."	"Listen! I hear the voice of my Beloved! Look! He is coming back to me, Easily leaping over every obstacle that stands between us."

VERSE 9:
"Behold, he standeth behind our wall, he looketh forth at the windows, shewing himself through the lattice."

He comes as close to us as possible. This wall is something that is hindering Him from coming closer. There are a couple of possibilities concerning this wall. Our sin presents a wall that He cannot penetrate. He looks at us through a window because He longs for closeness, for intimacy. Yet, He sees our sinful condition. He allows us to see Him through the lattice, which means He entices us with the possibility of closeness and intimacy. Once we confess our sins, He forgives us, fellowship is restored, and the wall between us comes down.

Another possibility concerning the wall is our schedule, our busyness, our obligations, and responsibilities. He looks in at the window longingly, desiring intimacy and closeness with us. Yet, He sees our busyness. He reveals Himself through the lattice, enticing us with the possibility of intimacy and closeness. My interpretation of verse 9:

KJV	MY VERSION
"Behold, he standeth behind our wall, he looketh forth at the windows, shewing himself through the lattice."	"He has stopped and is looking at me through the windows. I can see Him through the window panes."

VERSE 10:
"My beloved spake, and said unto me,
Rise up, my love, my fair one, and come away."

She tells us that Christ extended a verbal invitation to intimacy, a verbal call to go beyond the wall and the window. Whether the wall is one of sin or busyness, He calls us beyond it. He calls for us to turn from sin and enter into intimacy with Him. He has grace for your sin. He offers mercy, forgiveness, and the power to overcome sin. Sometimes grace for our sin involves deliverance, which He also offers.

He calls for us to rise out of busyness and answer His call of intimacy. He has grace for your schedule too. Grace means favor. If you take Him up on His offer of grace for your schedule, you will walk in favor with God and favor with man. Amazingly, this kind of favor can free up your schedule.

Christ called her "My love." *My* signifies that He is possessive of us. *Love* signifies that we are the objects of His affection. He also called her "My fair one." We see that possessive word *my* again. We belong to Him, and He doesn't want to share us with sin. He does not want to be second place on our schedule. Recall that *fair* means "to be bright, beautiful, alluring, desirable, and decked out." Remember, He compared us to lilies and said they are more glorious than Solomon's fine apparel. We are more glorious and beautiful than King Solomon in his finest clothes. Since Solomon is a picture of Christ, in some mysterious way He is saying that we are more glorious and beautiful than He is. That's pretty difficult to accept, but that's how He sees us.

He called for her to "come away." He wants us to come away from sin. To repent from sin is to go in the opposite direction. He wants us to come away from our busyness and make spending time with Him a priority.

He comes as close to us as He can, as close as our sin or schedule will allow. The rest is up to us. For more intimacy, we must rise and come away to Him. My rendition of verse 10 is as follows:

KJV	MY VERSION
"My beloved spake, and said unto me, Rise up, my love, my fair one, and come away."	"My Beloved speaks to me, *Rise up, My love, My fair one, and come away with Me.*"

VERSES 11–13:

"For, lo, the winter is past, the rain is over and gone;
The flowers appear on the earth; the time of the singing of birds is come,
and the voice of the turtle is heard in our land; The fig tree putteth forth
her green figs, and the vines with the tender grape give a good smell.
Arise, my love, my fair one, and come away."

Just as there are seasons on the earth, there are also seasons in our lives. Winter symbolizes a hard season. There are few flowers in winter. Some are dead; others appear dead. There are few birds because they migrate south in winter. There are few fruits, figs, or grapes. Winter is typically thought of as a season of hardship and barrenness. Jesus declares in this verse that winter is over! He calls for her (for us) to rise up out of hardship and barrenness. He calls for us to "come away" with Him. *Arise* is the same word Jesus used in Mark 5. Jairus' daughter was dead, and Jesus called out to her, "Arise." She did. We, too, could be dead. Dead in sin. Dead in hopelessness or discouragement. Dead in a winter season. He is calling for you to arise out of death, out of your winter season.

Wow! If I'm no longer in a season of death, I've entered a season of life, and it's an eternal season: life abundant on this earth and life everlasting in heaven.

When winter finally ends, spring comes. Spring is a season of life, flowers, and birds singing. Verse 13 mentions "the voice of the turtle." This is a reference to turtle doves singing, which symbolizes the offering of praise. In the spring, there is fruit again. As indicated by the "fig tree," it is a season of fruitfulness. On the whole, spring speaks of regeneration, the resurrection of nature. What appeared to be dead comes back to life. My interpretation of verses 11–13 where Jesus is calling us and making it possible to live, really live:

KJV	MY VERSION
"For, lo, the winter is past, the rain is over and gone; The flowers appear on the earth; the time of the singing of birds is come, and the voice of the turtle is heard in our land; The fig tree putteth forth her green figs, and the vines with the tender grape give a good smell. Arise, my love, my fair one, and come away."	*"The hard, barren season is over. Arise out of un-forgiveness, discouragement, despair, shame, sin, and busyness. Life and beauty have come to you. I hear the song of praise, worship, and devotion that you sing to Me. I see the fruit you are bearing and I smell your fragrance of life. Arise, My love, My fair one, and come away."*

VERSE 14:

"O my dove, that art in the clefts of the rock, in the secret places of the stairs, let me see thy countenance, let me hear thy voice; for sweet is thy voice, and thy countenance is comely."

He calls us doves signifying our beauty, our innocence, our inoffensiveness, and our harmlessness in Him. We are called doves especially for the turtledove's faithfulness to her mate portraying our faithfulness to Christ. Doves live in the clefts of the rocks. Think about Moses, who hid in the cleft of the rock so that he could behold part of God's glory. Christ is the very rock we hide in for safety. As long as we stay in Christ, we can see and experience God's glory.

"In the secret places of the stairs" refers to being hidden away, alone. Perhaps examining one's own heart in a place of personal reflection. Or perhaps a hiding place due to feeling unworthy. Or perhaps a hiding place due to sin, shame, fear, or unwillingness to forgive. This speaks of the ebb and flow of our relationship with Christ. He invites and begs you to come out of hiding from Him. He wants to see you. He enjoys your "countenance," your face, you. He enjoys you! He calls you *comely*, which means "beautiful." He wants to hear your voice praising Him and making requests. Your voice is sweet, pleasant, and agreeable. He calls you out of sin, shame, fear, and unworthiness. He desires to see you and hear you. He values what you have to say.

He's calling for us to get over our wounds and come out. He wants us to forgive. Lack of forgiveness hinders the maturing process. Intimacy is for grown-ups, for the mature. By coming out of offense, one is released to life, maturity, intimacy, and freedom. When you come out from under the stairs, you can climb up those stairs. You can get closer to Him. It's like a spiritual promotion, a going up. My interpretation of verse 14 looks like this:

KJV	MY VERSION
"O my dove, that art in the clefts of the rock, in the secret places of the stairs, let me see thy countenance, let me hear thy voice; for sweet is thy voice, and thy countenance is comely."	"O My devoted one, I see you hiding, thinking you are not fit to be seen, But I want to see your face. I long to see you. Let me hear your voice; for it is sweet and your face is beautiful."

VERSE 15:
"Take us the foxes, the little foxes, that spoil the vines: for our vines have tender grapes."

We are to violently oppose, capture, take, or deal with anything that would cause us to hide from Him, even little things, because they grow into big things just like little foxes grow into big foxes. The fox symbolizes sinful appetites and passions, even little, seemingly harmless ones. Fear is a fox that destroys the vine and its fruit. Fear will cause you to hide, to hold back, to hesitate. Fear paralyzes you. *Offense* is another fox. The lies of the enemy are like sly foxes. Shame, rejection, and unworthiness are all foxes that destroy the vine and its fruit.

Foxes spoil the vine by devouring the fruit. The vineyard symbolizes the Christian's soul or perhaps the Christian's character. If foxes are running around, there is little fruit in a person's life. Foxes are tricky and deceitful. They skulk, lurk, and hide in holes. So does your sin, your fear, and the lies you believe. They hide and cause you to think all is well while they destroy your fruit. These must be exposed by prayerful and diligent self-examination. Take them, drag them out of their holes, and expose them to the full judgment of God. Confess them. Repent of them. Destroy them before they destroy you. I love that He is in this with us. He says, "Take us the foxes." It is only with His help that we overcome these foxes. My presentation of verse 15:

KJV	MY VERSION
"Take us the foxes, the little foxes, that spoil the vines: for our vines have tender grapes."	*"Let's capture and take the insecurities, sins, lies, and all that stands between us. Let's capture even the little things, so that nothing spoils our intimacy, or destroys the fruit that we bare together."*

I titled this portion of chapter 2: Come Away. Jesus desires intimacy with you so much that He calls out to you, "come away." The Lord is calling us away from worldly distractions into intimacy with Himself. He offers us freedom from the foxes (insecurities, lies, sin, shame, and bitterness) that torment and hinder us. As you reread the translated verses altogether, answer His call and take Him up on His offer of freedom.

Reflection and Response

What foxes are hiding in your life, destroying fruit and wreaking havoc where there should be peace? Maybe your foxes are fear, depression, sin, shame, guilt, lack of forgiveness, or just plain busyness. Expose it to Jesus, and let Him bring you out of that winter season into a greater awareness of His love, acceptance, and presence. Respond to His call: "Come away." Afterward, record how He ministered to you.

_____

_____

_____

_____

_____

_____

_____

_____

WEEK TWO

Song of Solomon 2:16–17

POSSESSION

Remember, she was behind the wall, hiding from Him because of busyness, sin, shame, fear, woundedness, lack of forgiveness, or lies of the enemy. He called to her and starting at verse 16, she responds.

VERSE 16:
"My beloved is mine, and I am his: he feedeth among the lilies."

He is mine, and I am His. Sin is no longer between them. Busyness is not between them. The foxes have been taken and judged. Their intimacy is restored. They possess each other. Think about that for a few minutes. Fully give yourself to Him. He wants to possess you. You can possess Him.

She rejoices that "He feeds among the lilies." Remember way back in verse 2: He calls us lilies among thorns. Now, this verse says that He feeds among the lilies. He feeds among us. He feeds on us. He is satisfied with something in this world. Wow, it's me. My intimacy with Him and my praises and worship satisfy Him, they feed Him. He takes pleasure in me. I quench his thirst. Here is my presentation of verse 16:

KJV	MY VERSION
"My beloved is mine, and I am his: he feedeth among the lilies."	"My Beloved is mine, and I am His. I possess Him and He possesses me. He enjoys and finds great satisfaction in me."

VERSE 17:

"Until the day break, and the shadows flee away, turn, my beloved, and be thou like a roe or a young hart upon the mountains of Bether."

She looks forward to the day when Christ returns for the church because that day will change everything. Then they will always be together. She asks Him that until that day He "turn" to her and come to her like a roe on the mountains. Mountains are things that separate. *Mountains of Bether* refers to an actual place that was very craggy (Strong). It symbolizes the world. She prays, "Don't let the world be an obstacle between us but come to me, my Beloved." Here is my rendition of verse 17:

KJV	MY VERSION
"Until the day break, and the shadows flee away, turn, my beloved, and be thou like a roe or a young hart upon the mountains of Bether."	"Jesus, my Beloved, Until the day comes that we can be together always, come often to me, climbing over and breaking through every obstacle to get to me."

This was a short lesson today, but it conveys the profound truth of mutual possession. Jesus delights in and finds satisfaction in intimacy with you. He will do whatever it takes to get to you. As you reread the translated verses altogether, speak them to Jesus. Go for it. Jesus will be thrilled!

Reflections

To what extent do you feel like He is yours? To what extent do you feel like you are His? How so?

_____

_____

_____

_____

How do you feel about the fact that He feeds (is satisfied) on intimacy with you?

_____

_____

_____

Response

Prepare a meal for Him. Feed Him—satisfy Him. Worship Him and love on Him.

Record your encounter with Him.

WEEK TWO

Song of Solomon 2

RISE UP

My final thoughts about chapter 2: When I was pregnant with my first child, my husband and I had a water bed. As I grew larger, it became very difficult for me to get out of that bed. You can probably imagine me trying and straining to bend my middle so I could get out of bed. It was very comical, but it was getting serious. I truly could not get out of bed without assistance! My wonderful husband attached a rope from the ceiling that hung down at arm's length so that I could grab hold of it and pull myself up. I used it to "rise up."

Get a hold of the Lord and rise up. Get a hold of His Word and rise up. Pull yourself up out of hopelessness, fear, depression, sin, shame, guilt, unworthiness, woundedness, bitterness, and unforgiveness. Get a hold of the truth and rise up!

Enjoy the following rendition of Song of Solomon 2 in which I have replaced the symbolism and the metaphors with words that demonstrate His love and heart for us. Once again Jesus' words are in italics.

"I am the desired, beautiful, fragrant One.
My grace, mercy, and love are accessible and available to all.
I am pure, humble, and I am Life.
You, My love, are alive, desired, beautiful,
fragrant, valuable, and pure in Me.
You dwell among filthy, wicked, hurtful, noxious lost ones.
You dwell among hardship and danger and yet you thrive.
There is no one else like my Beloved.
His covering protects me and keeps me safe.
I rest in the shadow of His cross.
I am secure in His saving grace.
I love all that He offers me.
It's a banquet of life, beauty, grace,
mercy, purity, love, and salvation.
He leads and helps me over every obstacle
into deeper intimacy with Himself,
Into the fullness of His love, which is better than wine.
My heart is made glad and light.
His love covers me, protects me and secures victory for me.
Oh Jesus, press down on me until we are one,
And continue pressing
until You have become the foundation of my life.
Comfort me with grace and mercy.
For I am all together overcome by Your love.
He is holding me now
for I have fallen under the power and glory of His love.
His left hand is under my head,
and His right-hand embraces me.
I command my heart, my mind, even my friends to be still.
Do not disturb my Beloved!
Be still for He is easily disturbed
and will flee away from our intimate time.

Listen! I hear the voice of my Beloved!
Look! He is coming back to me.
Easily leaping over every obstacle that stands between us.
He has stopped and is looking at me through the windows.
I can see Him through the windowpanes.
My Beloved speaks to me,
Rise up, My love, My fair one, and come away with Me.
The hard, barren season is over.
Arise out of unforgiveness, discouragement,
despair, shame, sin, and busyness.
Life and beauty have come to you.
I hear the song of praise, worship, and devotion
that you sing to Me.
I see the fruit you are bearing and I smell your fragrance of life.
Arise, My love, My fair one, and come away.
O My devoted one,
I see you hiding, thinking you are not fit to be seen,
But I want to see your face. I long to see you.
Let me hear your voice; for it is sweet and your face is beautiful.
Let's capture and take the insecurities, sins, lies,
and all that stands between us.
Let's capture even the little things,
So that nothing spoils our intimacy,
or destroys the fruit that we bare together.
My beloved is mine, and I am His.
I possess Him and He possesses me.
He enjoys and finds great satisfaction in me.
Jesus, my Beloved,
Until the day comes that we can be together always,
Come often to me,
Climbing over and breaking through
every obstacle to get to me."

Reflection and Response

If you are doing this as a group Bible study, use day five as the day you come together. Go over the refection questions from each day together. Share, encourage and pray for one another.

_____

_____

_____

_____

_____

If you are doing this study on your own, review the reflection and response sections from each day. Worship Him and ask Him to do a deeper work. Ask Him to add another layer of truth and beauty to your heart. Afterward, record your experience with Him here.

_____

_____

_____

_____

_____

_____

WEEK THREE

Song of Solomon 3:1–2

A LONELY SOUL ON A DARK NIGHT

These two verses are loaded with words that conjure up images of sexual desire. Words like *night*, *bed*, *sought*, and *love*. Let me repeat that this is not a physical sexual seeking. How does God want us to apply this portion of His word? Let's dissect it verse by verse, word by word and find out. I love going deeper into the Word. I hope you do too.

VERSE 1:
"By night on my bed I sought him whom my soul loveth:
I sought him, but I found him not."

The word *soul* points to the mind, will, and emotions. The soul loves Him. This is a matter of the soul. It is night, and this soul should be sleeping. However, the well-being of your mind, the contentment of your will, and the quietness of your emotions are all necessary for you to rest. This should be a season rest, but the Prince of Peace is absent, and this soul cannot rest.

Night, or a night season, refers to a season of darkness, a season of not being able to see what's ahead, of being lost on your journey. It could refer to a lack of vision or a lack of direction. It's a season of questions and questioning. It's a lonely season, a fearful season, a season of desperation. A restless soul affects the spirit and even the body. Check out Psalm 77:2 where David describes his night season.

How do we get in a night season? How did this person go from receiving salvation in chapter 1 and drawing closer to Him in chapter 2 into this night season? There are several possibilities. The first being personal sin. Or, perhaps this is a spiritual test or trial. Did you ever notice that the teacher is quiet during a test? Often when we are in a trial, it seems as though God does not speak to us. He is quiet. A third possibility is that the enemy is blocking the light, thus the night season is of the enemy's making.

The bed indicates this should be a time of rest, a time of intimacy with the Savior. But the mind is tormented. The will is restless. The emotions are troubled. Why? Because the Savior is not there. The soul must seek Him. Isaiah tells us that the seeking must be done at an acceptable time (Isaiah 55:6), and Jeremiah tells us that the seeking must be done with all the heart (Jeremiah 29:13). My interpretation of verse 1:

KJV	MY VERSION
"By night on my bed I sought him whom my soul loveth: I sought him, but I found him not."	"I looked for Him, but it was very dark. I just couldn't find Him. I rose up and I went searching for Him."

VERSE 2:

"I will rise now, and go about the city in the streets,
and in the broad ways I will seek him whom my soul loveth:

I sought him, but I found him not. Rise out of complacency. Become an active, determined, persistent seeker—a seeker that cries out like blind Bartimaeus. He was desperate to see. He had no pride left. Bartimaeus cried out, "Jesus, thou son of David, have mercy on me" (Luke 18:38).

Rise out of sin. Repent. Rise out of pride or self-sufficiency. Rise out of what others will think if they see you with Him. If this is a test or trial, rise like the eagle who soars over the storms of life. If this is a block from your enemy, rise like a warrior against the forces of darkness. Whatever it is you're facing, rise and overcome through Christ.

She looked for Him in the city. The city was Jerusalem, which is a type and shadow of the church (Henry). The church is a good place to look for Jesus (Luke 2:46).

This bride looked for Him "in the streets," which refers to the activities of the church (Henry). She looked for Him "in the broad ways," which refers to ritualism or tradition (Henry). Activities, programs, religion, ritualism, and tradition keep you busy and are often worth your time, but they can distract you from real intimacy with Jesus. He cannot be found in activities or programs. He cannot be found in religion, legalism, ritualism, or tradition. My rendition of verse 2 is as follows:

KJV	MY VERSION
"I will rise now, and go about the city in the streets, and in the broad ways, I will seek him whom my soul loveth: I sought him, but I found him not."	"I looked in the church, in its ways of religion and legalism; I looked for Him in the broad ways of the church through ritualism and traditions; But I did not find Him whom my soul loves. I felt empty and alone."

Friends, I'm so sorry that we are ending day one on such a sad note. This soul is still lonely and in a dark season. Some of you may be able to relate all too well. If so, I encourage you to be honest about where you are and how you feel. Take some extra time to record your feelings in the reflection and response sections. And hold on, because we will see in tomorrow's lesson that things turn around quickly. For now, go back and reread the translated verses altogether.

Reflections

Share about a night season you've experienced, maybe a time that you felt lonely or deserted.

_____
_____
_____
_____

Read Luke 10:38-42. To what extent are you the type of person who prefers to be busy over sitting still with the Lord?

Response

Spend some time just sitting with Him. Talk to Him about the reflection questions. Record your experience with Him.

WEEK THREE

Song of Solomon 3:3–5

DESPERATION

I'm anxious to find out what happened. Did she ever find Jesus? Where did she find Jesus? Why was it so hard to find Him?

VERSE 3:
"The watchmen that go about the city found me: to whom I said, Saw ye him whom my soul loveth?"

This lonely seeking soul is found by the watchmen of the city and asks if the watchmen know where her lover (Jesus) is. In Bible times, the watchmen of a city were positioned high on the walls of the city to watch over its safety. They constantly looked in the city and outside the city walls to make sure all was well. At the sight of threat, the watchmen would sound an alarm to warn the city and activate its troops.

Once again, the city refers to Jerusalem and is a foreshadow of the church. Spiritual watchmen are positioned in the spirit so they see things concerning the church. They see by prophecy, visions, and dreams.

They see, know, discern, and perceive in the spirit. Here is my interpretation of verse 3:

KJV	MY VERSION
"The watchmen that go about the city found me: to whom I said, Saw ye him whom my soul loveth?"	"The prophets and seers of the church found me so, I asked them, 'Do you know where my Jesus is? I love Him, I need Him, but I cannot find Him.'"

VERSE 4: "
It was but a little that I passed from them,
but I found him whom my soul loveth."

The verse continues, but I want you to notice something here. The seeker asks the watchmen for help and then finds Jesus. Often, prophetic people can see the problem and tell you the reason you cannot find Him. Whether it is sin, pride, prayerlessness, neglect of scripture, a test, or the enemy, a prophetic word can help you. Don't be afraid of prophets or the Word of the Lord through them. The guidance and admonition of a true seer prophet will line up with the written Word of God.

VERSE 4:
"It was but a little that I passed from them,
but I found him whom my soul loveth: I held him,
and would not let him go, until I had brought him
into my mother's house, and into the chamber of her
that conceived me."

She "held him and would not let him go" makes me think of 1 Thessalonians 5:21: "Hold fast that which is good." Through trials, struggles, storms, depression, sickness, death, darkness, and any other night season, hold onto Him! Hold on to your faith in Him! Whatever night season comes, hold on to Jesus! Don't let go and have to go searching for Him.

Next, we read "I brought him to my mother's house, into the room where I was conceived." This seems like a strange thing to do. She was desperate to get to the root of the problem. Many times, the night season in your life will repeat itself until you take Jesus to your mother's house even to the room and time of your conception. This is talking about dealing with generational sins and curses. "The Lord is longsuffering, and of great mercy, forgiving iniquity and transgression, and by no means clearing the guilty, visiting the iniquity of the fathers upon the children unto the third and fourth generation" (Numbers 14:18).

Many times, the reason for your night season and inability to rest is found in generational issues. These issues will keep reoccurring until you deal with the generational roots. Bring Jesus to your ancestors, both on your mother's side and your father's side back to the fourth generation. Even the circumstances of your conception and your time in the womb bear weight on who you are and your spiritual struggles. The Word tells us that He knew us when we were in the womb (Psalm 139:13). Take Him there and ask Him who you are? Ask Him to restore that person, so that His plans for you (Jeremiah 29:11) can come to pass.

Do not neglect this in your spiritual journey. You begin with salvation and progress to Holy Spirit Baptism. The Word says add precept upon precept. Do not leave this one out. Take Him to your mother's house. It is important and necessary! Here is my interpretation of verse 4:

KJV	MY VERSION
"It was but a little that I passed from them, but I found him whom my soul loveth: I held him, and would not let him go, until I had brought him into my mother's house, and into the chamber of her that conceived me."	"After talking to the prophets, I found my Love. I held Him, and would not let Him go, until He and I dealt thoroughly with my generational issues, even the circumstances of my conception."

VERSE 5:

"I charge you, O ye daughters of Jerusalem, by the roes, and by the hinds of the field, that ye stir not up, nor awake my love, till he please."

Quiet yourself: spiritually, mentally, emotionally, and physically. Symbolically, stay with Jesus in your mother's house, in the bed of your conception until He says it's finished. Take all the time necessary. *Roes* and *hinds* refer to deer who frighten easily and run away. Don't run! Stay in this place with Jesus. Trust Him on the journey into your past. He will bring you to a place of spiritual rest and restoration. I present my rendition of verse 5:

KJV	MY VERSION
"I charge you, O ye daughters of Jerusalem, by the roes, and by the hinds of the field, that ye stir not up, nor awake my love, till he please."	"I commanded my heart, my mind, even my friends to be still. Be still for He is easily disturbed and will flee away from me. Do not disturb my Beloved! My Love will stir when the work in me is finished."

The lonely seeking soul found relief and help. God is so faithful! Jesus is but a prayer away and always eager to come to your rescue. I think there are several valuable truths in today's lesson. I want to recap the lesson by reviewing two of them.

First and foremost: Once you find Jesus, hold on and don't let go! Through trials, struggles, storms, depression, sickness, death, darkness, and any other night season hold on to Him! Hold on to your faith in Him! "Hold fast that which is good" (1 Thessalonians 5:21).

Second: Don't be afraid of exploring generation sins and curses with Jesus. He only wants to set you free, heal, and restore you. You do this in prayer. You bring Jesus to your ancestors on both sides of your family. Repent on behalf of your ancestors for any generational sins. In Jesus' name and by His blood in your life, break the curses off your life as a result of those sins. Bring Him to the time of your conception as well. Ask Him who He intended you to be. Ask Him to restore that person so that His plans for you can come to pass. I cannot stress how important this is in your relationship with Jesus. You may want some additional material on the subject of generation sins and curses. I recommend: *Restoring the Foundations* by Chester and Betsy Kylstra (www.restoringthefoundations.org/). If you do not deal with these issues, you will eventually hit a wall in your relationship with Him and will not be able to go completely into the future He has planned for you. Truly putting these issues behind you will allow you to go forward in life with greater boldness and victory.

As you go back through the lesson to reread the translated verses, know that Jesus wants to heal any wounded areas of your life that hinder your relationship with Him.

Reflections

In what area of your life are you desperate for a breakthrough?

_____

_____

_____

To what extent do you think generational sins and curses might be impacting your life?

_____

_____

_____

How do you feel about exploring these issues? (If you have already dealt with generation sins and curses, perhaps you want to share with the group and encourage others to pursue healing, forgiveness, and freedom from generational sins and curses.)

_____

_____

_____

_____

Response

Symbolically, invite Jesus to your mother's house. Talk to Him about your conception, your upbringing, any generational diseases, and any generation sin patterns you may be aware of. Ask Him to show you generational sin patterns that you are not aware of. According to Psalm 139:13, He knew you in the womb. Ask Him who you are. Ask Him to heal, deliver, and restore you so that you can be the person He intended. Record your time with Jesus here.

_____

_____

_____

_____

_____

_____

_____

_____

_____

_____

WEEK THREE

Song of Solomon 3:6–8

INTIMACY RESTORED

The scene changes drastically. She was resting with Jesus in her mother's bed, where she was being held by Him and restored to His plans for her life. In His arms, generational sins and curses were cut off so that they no longer affected her. But now we are looking at some kind of wilderness and then King Solomon's bed. So, let's dive in and figure out what this passage is talking about.

VERSE 6:
"Who is this that cometh out of the wilderness like pillars of smoke, perfumed with myrrh and frankincense, with all powders of the merchant?"

I love this verse! At first glance, most readers identify this as Christ. And it could refer to Christ. Remember His experience in the wilderness when tempted by the devil. Jesus came out of that wilderness experience victorious. Some might remember Israel, how the nation wandered in the wilderness for forty years but then emerged to possess the promised land.

But this passage is about you and me. By taking Him to our roots, our ancestors, and our conception, His fragrance rubs off on us. His fragrance transforms even our wilderness times, dark times, hurtful times, desperate night seasons, and the lonely times into something we come out of bearing His fragrance and beauty. This is where the work of Isaiah 61 is done in our lives.

"(He gave me) Beauty for ashes, the oil of joy for mourning, the garment of praise for the spirit of heaviness, (WHY) that we might be trees of righteousness, the planting of the Lord, that He might be glorified" (Isaiah 61:3, parenthesis mine).

So, this is you coming out of the wilderness, like pillars of smoke (powerful in the Lord), perfumed with myrrh and frankincense and powders (His fragrance all over you). You can see why I love this verse! This pillar of smoke also speaks of a burnt offering. It speaks of dying to self. It speaks of the crucifixion of our flesh. Just as Jesus' body was anointed with all kinds of spices, when we embrace the death of our flesh, we take on His fragrance, which rises and becomes a sweet savor to Him and even to others. Below is my rendition of verse 6:

KJV	MY VERSION
"Who is this that cometh out of the wilderness like pillars of smoke, perfumed with myrrh and frankincense, with all powders of the merchant?"	"Who is that coming out of the wilderness so powerfully? Smelling like death, yet alive and smelling wonderful? It's me! I've come out of the dark season. I've come out victorious and smelling like Him. His scent is all over me."

Verse 6 indicates that the wife or bride is getting all this attention because she has come out of the wilderness in victory. But notice what she does with that attention. She immediately (in verse 7) diverts everyone's attention from herself to the reason for her victory:

VERSE 7:
"Behold his bed, which is Solomon's;
threescore valiant men are about it,
of the valiant of Israel."

The Old Testament is full of types and shadows. Most commentaries agree that Solomon was a type of Christ and Solomon's many wives were a type of the church with its many denominations. This verse literally refers to Solomon's bed. Just as King Solomon was intimate with each of his wives, each of us can be intimate with Christ.

Song of Solomon 1:13 says that Christ "lies between my breasts all night." This sounds very sensual, but think about what organ lies between the breast. It's your heart. Christ's bed is the heart of the believer. That's where intimacy takes place—in your heart. Not in the organ that pumps blood but in your spirit.

VERSES 7 AND 8:
"Behold his bed, which is Solomon's; threescore valiant men are about it,
of the valiant of Israel. They all hold swords, being expert in war:
every man hath his sword upon his thigh because of fear in the night."

King Solomon and his wives would have been well guarded each night by the best and bravest warriors at the king's disposal. We can enter into intimacy with Christ, knowing that we are safe in His arms and that heaven's angels are camped around us (Psalm 34:7). Security and peace of mind can be found in His bed. Intimacy with Christ brings us to a place of spiritual rest. My presentation of verses 7 and 8 follows:

KJV	MY VERSION
"Behold his bed, which is Solomon's; threescore valiant men are about it, of the valiant of Israel. They all hold swords, being expert in war: every man hath his sword upon his thigh because of fear in the night."	"Look at Jesus. Look at and consider intimacy with Him. You will be safe with Him. Warring angels surround those who are intimate with Him. They are ready to protect you. Do not be afraid of intimacy with Jesus."

Let's think about how this chapter has progressed. At the beginning of the chapter, the woman's soul had no rest; she could not sleep. Generational issues tormented her mind, tore at her will, and put her emotions in upheaval. After allowing Christ to deal with the generational issues, she finds herself in Christ's bed! Rest and peace come from being in His arms, from being intimate with Him.

Go back now and reread the translated verses where we uncovered who it is that's coming out of the wilderness in victory. It's you and me!

Reflections

How does this encourage you to step into greater intimacy with Christ?

_____

_____

_____

What does "coming out the wilderness" mean for you?

___

Response

Worship Jesus. Press into the safe place of His loving arms. Be completely vulnerable with Him. You can trust Him. Record your experience with Him here.

WEEK THREE

Song of Solomon 3:9–11

A CHARIOT RIDE

The bride is still talking in these verses, pointing others to Jesus, telling others to trust Him with their hearts, encouraging others to step into deeper intimacy with Him. She explains that He made a way by providing a chariot that will take us to places of deeper intimacy and so much more. Let's find out about this chariot and what it represents.

VERSE 9:

"King Solomon made himself a chariot of the wood of Lebanon."

Matthew Henry wrote that this chariot may represent the human nature of Christ riding in His divine nature. Other commentaries offer the chariot as the gospel, which brings Christ to us and us to our heavenly Father.

After much study and prayer over this verse, I concluded that this chariot is a picture of the gospel, of Christ's work and the surety of where it will take us. Not just to heaven though. It will take us into all that

God has for us, into the full and abundant life that Jesus provides for us (John 10:10).

In the Old Testament, chariots are associated with the splendor and riches of a king. The gospel does bring us a glorious king, King Jesus. A King that makes us rich with the blessings of God. Old Testament chariots are also associated with war, such as a conquering king. Christ is a conquering King. He triumphed over sin and death for us. We can ride with Him into victory regarding the issues of our lives.

This chariot was made from the "wood of Lebanon." The wood from Lebanon is said to have eternal qualities; it will never rot (Henry). Christ was crucified on a wooden cross. The work of His cross will stand for eternity. The wood from Lebanon was expensive. The wooden cross of Christ cost Him everything. He paid that price for us. Here is my interpretation of verse 9:

KJV	MY VERSION
"King Solomon made himself a chariot of the wood of Lebanon."	"Jesus made a way for you to come to Him. You come to Him by way of the wooden cross He died on."

VERSE 10:
"He made the pillars thereof of silver, the bottom thereof of gold, the covering of it of purple, the midst thereof being paved with love, for the daughters of Jerusalem."

Silver represents His Word. The Bible says "the words of the Lord are as silver tried" (Psalm 12:6). That means we can trust in His Word. It's been tried over and over again. The Word won't fail us. We can also trust in these pillars of silver. These pillars are strong and will not be shaken! Just as the Word never fails and always accomplishes His desire, so will these silver pillars. We need the pillars of His Word. That's what will carry us through to our destiny. "Pillars of silver" is a reference to the seven pillars mentioned in Proverbs 9:1, indicating true wisdom. Wisdom will keep us and carry us to our destiny.

The bottom of the chariot was gold, real gold. Gold is the longest lasting metal. It has eternal qualities. It speaks of having a solid and eternal foundation in Christ. To me, the silver and the gold speak of "the unsearchable *riches* of Christ" (Ephesians 3:8). "We have redemption through His blood, the forgiveness of sins, according to the *riches* of His grace" (Ephesians 1:7). Paul prayed, "That the eyes of our understanding would be enlightened; that we would know what is the hope of His calling, and what is the *riches* of the glory of His inheritance in the saints" (Ephesians 1:8). Yes, the gospel brings Christ to us, and it brings us to unsearchable riches in Him.

Solomon's chariot is covered with purple, which probably refers to purple curtains (Henry). Purple is symbolic of the color of blood (Henry). Just as Solomon's covering of purple curtains protected whoever was riding in the chariot from winds and storms, the blood covering of Christ protects the believer from the winds and storms of God's wrath. The blood covering of Christ protects the believer from the attacks of the enemy (Revelation 12:11).

I love this next part. Solomon's chariot was paved with love. This is how you know, beyond doubt, that this book is an allegory and that Solomon is a type of Christ. How can an actual chariot be paved with love? It's the gospel that's paved with love.

There is a progression concerning this chariot. The base was wood, expensive wood, but the value progressed. Silver is better than wood, gold is better than silver, blood is better than gold, and love is better than blood. His love is such a valuable treasure! I challenge you: Don't settle for salvation. Press into His love.

VERSE 10 (again):

"He made the pillars thereof of silver, the bottom thereof of gold, the covering of it of purple, the midst thereof being paved with love, for the daughters of Jerusalem."

The chariot was made for "the daughters of Jerusalem." That's you and me. That includes all believers (male and female), individually and collectively as the church. This chariot was a gift of love. It is the Gospel of Christ.

Think of that chariot and all the words used to describe it: wood, silver, gold, purple, and love. Now think about all the gifts of love you have received in your life. Maybe you received an item made of wood, like an expensive jewelry box or perhaps even a house. Exquisite silver jewelry is often a gift of love. Wedding rings are usually gold to signify that the marriage will last. A beautiful purple scarf would qualify as a gift of love, or perhaps a card with a purple heart on it. Maybe you received purple flowers that communicate, "I love you." All of these gifts of love pale in comparison to His love for you.

This chariot paved with His love will take you to your destiny in Him. His love for you will take you places. Just like a suitor takes a lady on a date. Just like a groom takes his bride on a honeymoon. Just like a husband takes his wife out to dinner. Christ will take you places that you would never have gone without Him. He unselfishly loves you and takes you places that fulfill the desires of your heart. He takes you to places that fulfill the call of God on your life. I am talking about the ride of your life. Not just a chariot ride to heaven, as wonderful as that is. This is the ride of your wildest dreams. You are going somewhere in and with Christ, and it looks like a cloud of glory.

Do you understand why God chose to communicate His love for us through an allegory? I think it's because mankind (males in particular) would never understand the passion that Christ has for us and the intimacy He desires to have with us unless it is presented in these sensual terms. Read my rendition of verse 10:

KJV	MY VERSION
"He made the pillars thereof of silver, the bottom thereof of gold, the covering of it of purple, the midst thereof being paved with love, for the daughters of Jerusalem."	"In His Word are pillars of truth and wisdom that will take you to your destiny. He is the foundation of your journey. Your adventure with Him will last for eternity, because it is covered by His blood, and made accessible by His love for you."

VERSE 11:

"Go forth, O ye daughters of Zion, and behold king Solomon with the crown where with his mother crowned him in the day of his espousals, and in the day of the gladness of his heart."

Go forth. Now that you know about the chariot, the gospel, go forth! Go forth from sin. Go forth from the world, leaving your worldly ways behind. Go forth from religion and dead works. Go forth from generational sins and curses. A way has been made for you to go forward into your destiny! Go forward. We are told to go forward and behold Him. Just look at Him and you will adore Him.

This reminds me of a time when my daughter was an infant. The two of us went to a clinic to get her immunizations. Sitting in the waiting room, I placed her carrier on the floor and positioned her so that she could see me. After waiting a long time, I said to her, "Hey, my sweetie, aren't you getting tired of looking at Mommy?" She smiled one of her first smiles. A lady sitting near me said, "She will be content to look at you for a long time." That's how we are when we look at Jesus, content to look at Him. Satisfied by Him. It is during these times of gazing on our Savior that we are changed into His image (2 Corinthians 3:18).

The next part of verse 11 tells us to look at his crown, the one his mother gave him on his wedding day. This is referring to King Solomon's coronation. The day of his coronation, the day of he was crowned king, was also his wedding day. On that day, his mother, Bathsheba, put his father's crown upon him to show that he would now be king. The day that he became king and got married would be a "day of gladness for him." How does all that relate to Christ? To us? God crowned Jesus with glory and honor, gave Him a seat in heaven, and placed all things under is feet (Ephesians 1:20–22). When an individual accepts Jesus and the work of the cross into their lives, it is the day of Christ's coronation in their heart and soul. It is the day they crown Him King of their lives. It is the day they begin to lay their crowns at His feet. This is the day that He is glad in His heart and rejoices over you and receives you as His betrothed. Read my interpretation of verse 11:

KJV	MY VERSION
"Go forth, O ye daughters of Zion, and behold king Solomon with the crown wherewith his mother crowned him in the day of his espousals, and in the day of the gladness of his heart."	"Go forward into all that He has for you. Behold King Jesus, Crowned with glory and honor. Believe in Him. Become His. Crown Him with your adoration and worship. Make His heart glad."

Press into intimacy with Him. Don't be robbed by the enemy. Satan will tell you not to bother pressing into Christ because you are not worthy. Just agree with your adversary and confess, "I'm not worthy, but I'm covered by His blood. He bled for intimacy with me. He loves me!" As you reread my presentation of verses 9–11, let the words come from your heart and crown Him with the worship He deserves.

Reflections

What does Solomon's chariot mean to you?

_____

_____

_____

_____

_____

Are you fully in the chariot of His love, ready to "go forth"? What are you going forth from? What are you going forth to?

_____

_____

_____

_____

_____

Response

Climb completely into that chariot of His love and let Him escort you into your future. He has great plans for you! "For I know the plans I have for you, declares the Lord, plans to prosper you and not harm you, plans to give you hope and a future" (Jeremiah 29:11, NIV). Record your thoughts as He ministers to you.

_____

_____

_____

_____

_____

_____

_____

_____

_____

_____

_____

WEEK THREE

Song of Solomon 3:1–11

JESUS REALLY DOES LOVES ME

We all know the children's song "Jesus Loves Me," yet we're not able to *love* the way He loves us. We have no capacity for that kind of love. His love gave all and is still giving. Below, I present my interpretation of Song of Solomon 3 in its entirety. The bride is talking throughout this chapter. I hope you enjoy it.

> "I looked for Him, but it was very dark.
> I just couldn't find Him.
> I rose up and I went searching for Him.
> I looked in the church, in its ways of religion and legalism;
> I looked for Him in the broad ways of the church
> through ritualism and traditions;
> But I did not find Him whom my soul loves.
> I felt empty and alone.
> The prophets and seers of the church found me
> so I asked them,

'Do you know where my Jesus is?
I love Him, I need Him, but I cannot find Him.'
After talking to the prophets, I found my Love.
I held Him, and would not let Him go,
Until He and I dealt thoroughly with my generational issues,
Even the circumstances of my conception.
I commanded my heart, my mind, even my friends to be still.
Be still for He is easily disturbed and will flee away from me.
Do not disturb my Beloved!
My love will stir when the work in me is finished.
Who is that coming out of the wilderness so powerfully?
Smelling like death, yet alive and smelling wonderful?
It's me! I've come out of the dark season.
I've come out victorious and smelling like Him.
His scent is all over me.
Look at Jesus.
Look at and consider intimacy with Him.
You will be safe with Him.
Warring angels surround those who are intimate with Him.
They are ready to protect you.
Do not be afraid of intimacy with Him.
Jesus made a way for you to come to Him.
You come to Him by way of the wooden cross He died on.
In His Word are pillars of truth and wisdom
that will take you to your destiny.
He is the foundation of your journey.
Your adventure with Him will last for eternity,
because it is covered by His blood,
and made accessible by His love for you.
Leave sin and every hindering issue behind you.
Go forward into all that He has for you.

> Behold King Jesus, crowned with glory and honor.
> Believe in Him. Become His.
> Crown Him with your adoration and worship.
> Make His heart glad."

Reflection and Response

If you are doing this as a group Bible study, use day five as the day you come together. Go over the refection questions from each day together. Share, encourage, and pray for one another.

_____

_____

_____

If you are doing this study on your own, review the reflection and response sections from each day. Worship Him and ask Him to do a deeper work. Ask Him to add another layer of truth and beauty to your heart. Afterward, record your experience with Him here.

_____

_____

_____

_____

WEEK FOUR

Song of Solomon 4:1

LOOK AT YOURSELF

    Jesus, our bridegroom, does most of the talking in this chapter. This is a passionate chapter. It's full of symbolism and metaphors which make it hard to understand how to apply it in our lives. We're going to take two weeks to study this chapter because it has so much for us to consider. As we go through the study, realize this is how Christ sees you. This is how He feels about you.

<u>**VERSE 1**</u> *(1st phrase)*:
"Behold, thou art fair, my love;
behold, thou art fair."

Christ has so much affection for us that He calls you and me "my love." You are His love. I am His love. He calls us *fair*, which means "beautiful, the fairest, even the most pleasant." Think about how we are made in the image of God. "The beauty of the Lord our God is upon us" (Psalm 90:17). In Christ, we also have the "beauty of holiness" (Psalm 29:2; 96:9).

Behold is a call to notice and take note. It is not a call to others that they should notice her. It is a call to the bride; it is a call to us that we take notice of who we are. He says it twice indicating that this is a serious order, not just a suggestion. He wants us to consider and see ourselves as He does. The second "behold" is a demonstrative, which reveals emotion. It shows frustration. He is frustrated that we do not see ourselves as He does. We are beautiful. We are His love.

So, say this out loud: "He wants me to look at me." That's hard to do, isn't it? We distract ourselves as much as possible from focusing on ourselves. We try to stay busy and keep our minds occupied. It's even harder to think of Him focusing on us, locking His gaze on us. But He is gazing on us, and He delights in us.

Jesus has a purpose for this statement: "Behold, thou art fair, my love, behold thou art fair." It is not to flatter or plant pride in her. This is not Him fishing for compliments or hoping to receive praise in return. It is to encourage her. Whatever others think of her, she is beautiful. Whatever she thinks of herself, she is beautiful. He wants her to see value in herself, but not external value. To His eyes, external virtues would add nothing to her, and the lack of them would deprive her of nothing. He says this to help her see value in herself because of the beauty of His grace, which He has put on her.

Here's my rendition of this phrase:

KJV	MY VERSION
"Behold, thou art fair, my love; behold, thou art fair."	*"Look at yourself, My love, you are beautiful. Really look now, you are beautiful."*

VERSE 1 *(2nd phrase)*:
"Thou hast doves' eyes within thy locks."

In Matthew 3:16, John saw the Spirit of God in the form of a dove rest on Jesus. Doves symbolize the Holy Spirit. To have dove's eyes is to see with the eyes of the Holy Spirit, or to see in the spirit realm. The first mention of doves in the Bible is found in Genesis, where a dove brought Noah the green olive leaf. The olive is known for its oil, another symbol of the Holy Spirit, which is used for anointing. Jesus is saying that we have Holy Spirit anointed eyes. We need to believe Him and agree with Him. Pray to see in the spirit. Expect to see. See! See what? Start with yourself. See yourself. He said, "Behold." He is telling you how you look in the spirit. In the spirit, you are beautiful, even the most pleasant. You can only see this in the realm of the spirit.

Locks sound like bangs that need to be trimmed, like hair covering your eyes. The actual meaning of the word is "veil," the covering worn by a woman that diverted her eyes from men. Women were to look only at their husbands. A woman was to be seen only by her husband. This signifies that it pleases Christ when we look to Him only and not to idols or other crutches.

KJV	MY VERSION
"Thou hast doves' eyes within thy locks."	*"Your eyes, under that veil, please Me because you reserve them for My glances only. Since you reserve them for Me only, they see in the realm of the spirit, I can show you great and mighty things that you know not of."*

<u>VERSE 1</u> *(3rd phrase)*:
"Thy hair is as a flock of goats, that appear from mount Gilead."

This is hilarious! Christ is so romantic! Our hair reminds Him of goats! What could this mean? I started with the word *goats* and found that *Strong's Concordance* says *goats* are "goats." I had to dig and pray for revelation. The Old Testament lists animals as either clean or unclean. I found that goats are clean animals. They are useful for eating, milking, sacrifice, and for making clothing or tents out of their hair and hide. We are like goats in that we are useful to the Lord.

A shepherd knows how many goats he has. Why? It's because they represent his wealth. Matthew 10:30 says that the hairs of our head are numbered. Connect the following two thoughts: Our hair is like a flock of goats. He knows how many hairs we have just like a shepherd knows how many goats he has. This is speaking of our value. We make Him wealthy.

Mount Gilead was a rocky, craggy mountain where goats roamed (Henry). Goats are sure-footed on the rough terrain. The Bible says that in Him we are sure-footed. Proverbs 30:29–31 says goats are "comely going." *Comely* comes from a root word which means "beautiful, made well, sound, and successful." So, goats are beautiful coming or going. What makes them beautiful to the shepherd? Their value makes them a beautiful sight to the shepherd.

Let's recap this goat stuff. It is a clean animal. We are cleansed from our sins through Christ. The goat is useful and therefore valuable. Jesus sees us as clean, useful, valuable, and beautiful. Sure-footed in Him. Blessed coming and going (Deuteronomy 28:6).

Continuing with verse 1, let's consider the word *hair*. For a woman, hair is symbolic of glory (1 Corinthians 11:15). Hair is also a head covering. When Christ looks at us, He sees His glory on us. He sees His glory covering us. He wants us to see and be aware of His glory on ourselves. His glory is what makes us beautiful. This is the last part of verse 1 in my words:

KJV	MY VERSION
"Thy hair is as a flock of goats, that appear from mount Gilead."	*"My glory upon you is stunning. You are extremely valuable to Me. So valuable that all your hairs are numbered. Oh, yes, My beloved, you are clean and desirable, And very beautiful."*

That's just verse 1 of this incredibly romantic chapter. Jesus is so in love with you and with me. Personalize the translated verse and get drawn into a love affair with Him.

Reflections

How do you feel about Christ looking at you?

_____

_____

_____

_____

_____

_____

_____

To what extent do you believe that this is how you look in the realm of the spirit?

___

Response

Press into His love. Choose to believe that He cherishes and adores you. Obey Him. Look at yourself. Try to see what He sees. Describe what you see.

___

WEEK FOUR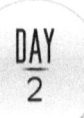

Song of Solomon 4:2–3

BRUSH YOUR TEETH

*I*n verse 1 Jesus compared us to goats. It's sheep in this verse. So romantic! Can you imagine anyone comparing their lover to goats or sheep?

VERSE 2:
"Thy teeth are like a flock of sheep that are even shorn, which came up from the washing; whereof every one bear twins, and none is barren among them."

Our teeth are compared to a whole flock of sheep that have been evenly and skillfully shaved for their wool. These sheep have also just been bathed and are followed by twin lambs, none of the sheep are barren. Oh my, what does all that say about us?

Teeth signify eating. Think about sheep. They eat grass. Sheep ruminate (regurgitate) the grass and chew it again for proper digestion. This is where we get the phrase "chew the cud."

Consider Matthew 4:4: "Man cannot live by bread alone but by every word which proceeds from the mouth of God." Just as the sheep ruminate the grass or cud and chew it again, we are to meditate on the Word of God or chew it again and again. This constant chewing on their cud makes the sheep's teeth even or "even shorn." Meditating on the Word makes our spiritual teeth even. It makes our theology balanced. Many teeth have names synonymous with wisdom: wisdom teeth, incisors (insight), and eyeteeth. Wisdom, which comes from meditating on the Word, makes us beautiful to the Lord.

These sheep "came up from the washing." They were washed, probably at a river, stream, or maybe a lake. This could speak of water baptism. This is a very important step in our Christian walk. It could also refer to Ephesians 5:26: "The washing of the water of the word." As we meditate on the Word, it cleanses our hearts and lives.

Now the phrase: "Everyone bears twins and none is barren among them." The teeth or the mouth speaks, declares, witnesses or testifies. This witnessing brings forth fruit or disciples. We are not spiritually barren. We reproduce for the Lord; we win people to Him. It says we not only reproduce but we also "bear twins." This refers to a double portion. Read my interpretation of verse 2:

KJV	MY VERSION
"Thy teeth are like a flock of sheep that are even shorn, which came up from the washing; whereof every one bear twins, and none is barren among them."	*"You've carefully balanced your life with wisdom; You have washed your soul with My Word, which has made you fruitful even to a double portion. You are not spiritually barren."*

VERSE 3 *(1st phrase)*:
"Thy lips are like a thread of scarlet, and thy speech is comely."

Scarlet indicates the color of crimson. In Bible times, cloth was died crimson using the blood of an animal. We can connect that with the blood of Jesus, but how does that tie in with our lips? Crimson or red lips indicate vibrant health. Pale lips indicate faintness, weakness, or infirmity. The Bible says our lips (our mouths) establish us in health and victory (Deuteronomy 30:19).

The bridegroom said, "Thy speech is comely." The words we say should be beautiful and lovely. We must realize the power of our words. We should be speaking positive things over others and ourselves. Your speech should be complementary to the work of Christ's blood (Revelation 12:11).

In verse 3, Jesus puts a lot of responsibility on us, showing us that the words we speak should line up with His word. My rendition of the first part of verse 3:

KJV	MY VERSION
"Thy lips are like a thread of scarlet, and thy speech is comely."	*"Your lips are beautifully stained with My blood. This is evident in your wise declarations of life."*

VERSE 3 *(2nd phrase)*:
"Thy temples are like a piece of a pomegranate within thy locks."

In Hebrew, the word *temples* can mean one of two things: a place on your head, just on the side of each eye, or the part of your face that we call the cheek. Which is it? The pomegranate gives us a clue.

A pomegranate is brownish-red on the outside, but when cut open, we see the inside is bright red. "A piece" would come from a sliced pomegranate, thus revealing the red. Matthew Henry believes "temples" must indicate the cheeks, since pomegranate seeds are red. So, we have Christ complimenting her red cheeks, which indicates a blushing, or innocence. This indicates humility and modesty. Here is my presentation of the last part of verse 3:

KJV	MY VERSION
"Thy temples are like a piece of a pomegranate within thy locks.	*"I see your humility and modesty Oh, how you please Me."*

We did it. We replaced all the symbolism and metaphors in this passage with words that make sense. Well kept, even teeth point to meditating on the Word and having a balanced theology. Bearing twins symbolizes the fruit we bear with our mouths. Scarlet lips are a picture of blood-stained lips or lips that speak what Jesus accomplished for us. Pomegranate-like temples under our locks are simply a portrait of our humility and modesty. Reread the translated verses and realize that Christ is speaking to you.

Reflections

What are some benefits of meditating on the Word?

_____

_____

_____

Why is it important that our words line up with the words and work of Christ?

Response

Spend some time with Him. Remember that He asking you to look at yourself. What is He showing you about yourself? Record your thoughts here.

WEEK FOUR

Song of Solomon 4:4–5

BATTLE READY YET COMPASSIONATE

*C*hrist continues to speak. He continues to describe what He sees when He looks at us. Remember that He wants you to see yourself this way. This time He is talking about your neck and your breasts. The question came to me, "What am I, a chicken?"

VERSE 4:
"Thy neck is like the tower of David builded for an armoury,
whereon there hang a thousand bucklers,
all shields of mighty men."

In this verse, *neck* is literal. It connects the body to the head, thus holding up the head. The neck is compared to a tower. You might remember seeing pictures of ancient Egyptian women with their necks wrapped to elongate them, causing them to look something like a tower. This look was perceived as elegant, beautiful, and royal.

The word *David* in this verse refers to the king of Israel and captain of its army. An armory is a place where weapons are stored. Scripture admonishes you to "arm your mind" with the "mind of Christ" (1 Peter 4:1; Romans 8:31, 35–37; 1 John 4:4). Memorize the word; store it up in your mind as a weapon and a shield. Your mind should contain 1000 bucklers, or shields. "Mighty men" refers to soldiers or heroes of war. Your mind can bring you into victory. Arm it well with the Word. My interpretation of verse 4 is as follows:

KJV	MY VERSION
"Thy neck is like the tower of David builded for an armoury, whereon there hang a thousand bucklers, all shields of mighty men."	*"Your lovely neck supports your mind which you have stocked piled as an armory with weapons that defeat the enemy. It contains a thousand shields, like the ones that belonged to David's mighty men."*

VERSE 5:
"Thy two breasts are like two young roes that are twins, which feed among the lilies."

The word *breasts* literally refers to a woman's breasts. Verses with such explicit sexual imagery require careful examination. We must always keep in mind that the physical, sexual images in this book should point us toward spiritual intimacy with Christ. Breasts are often associated with comfort, compassion, and even beauty. Breasts feed and nurture our children. Spiritually we are nurses to the children of God: feeding, teaching, and equipping them to live victoriously. Our breasts are compared to a young roe. A roe is a female deer, goat, or gazelle. Breasts that are "twins" speak of balance, meaning our theology (what we teach and feed others) is balanced. It is not lopsided or out in left field.

Our breasts "feed among the lilies." We saw this same phrase in chapter 2:16: "My beloved is mine, and I am His: He feeds among the lilies." Christ feeds among the lilies. If you meditate on this scripture, you will find that we are the lilies where Christ feeds. He nurtures Himself by and in fellowship with us. He doesn't need us, but He delights in us and chooses us. Chapter 4, verse 5 says we also feed among the lilies. If we feed among the lilies, this means we feed on Him, the lily of the valley. We are nurtured by fellowship with Him. This verse also means that we feed on fellowship with one another. This brings accountability and balance to our theology. The two breasts are twins because the theology is balanced. Out of this nurturing, we nurture others.

I want to make a connection between verses 4 and 5. My mind is an armory of weapons to defeat the enemy. All the time I spend in the Word, stockpiling weapons also makes my theology balanced. It also makes sense that who I fellowship with will affect my theology. My interpretation of verse 5 follows:

KJV	MY VERSION
"Thy two breasts are like two young roes that are twins, which feed among the lilies."	*"You beautifully demonstrate comfort, mercy, and compassion. With wisdom, you feed, nurture, and sustain those younger than yourself. You nourish yourself by feeding on Me and My body of believers."*

I'm amazed at the truths in this book of romance. Song of Solomon is often avoided because of the seemingly sexual content. Unless you study it deeply, it's hard to figure out what to do with it or how to apply it. I love finding out what it all means and especially discovering how much He loves me. I hope you do too! Go back and reread the translated verses and remember that Jesus is still speaking to you.

Reflections

Does your mind hold 1000 mighty shields? How can you add to your stockpile of weapons?

_____

_____

_____

_____

Before you got into this study, how did you respond to verses like verse 5 (verses and passages that talked about breasts)? In your own words, what do they symbolize?

_____

_____

_____

_____

Response

Spend some time worshiping Him and loving on Him. Let Him love on you. Remember that He wants you to look at yourself. What is He showing you? Write down what you see.

_____

_____

_____

_____

_____

_____

_____

_____

_____

_____

_____

_____

_____

WEEK FOUR

Song of Solomon 4:6–7

SPOTLESS

The groom is still speaking. Jesus is going somewhere. When we find out what the mountain of myrrh and the hill of frankincense symbolize, we will know where He is going.

VERSE 6:
*"Until the day break, and the shadows flee away,
I will get me to the mountain of myrrh,
and to the hill of frankincense."*

"Until the day break, and the shadows flee away" refers to the end of the day. The next part is a picture of where Jesus retires at the end of the day. Like most people, Jesus retires each day by going to the place where He lives. The "Mountain of myrrh" refers to Mt. Moriah, which is where the temple was in Solomon's day (Henry). This is where sacrifices and worship took place.

Myrrh and frankincense are incense. They were burnt daily in the temple. Myrrh is a sacred oil that releases a fragrant perfume when burned. Frankincense is also a fragrant incense. Incense is symbolic of our prayers and worship. God inhabits the praises of His people. So, this is a place where God's presence dwells. Jesus is saying that He chooses our hearts as His temple or resting place because of our worship and our prayers, and because of the fragrance released by them. Our prayers and worship are like a fragrant perfume that lure Him. I interpret verse 6 like this:

KJV	MY VERSION
"Until the day break, and the shadows flee away, I will get me to the mountain of myrrh, and to the hill of frankincense."	*"I am very pleased with your fragrance, My beloved; I delight in your worship and prayers. I choose your heart of worship as My resting place and My abode."*

VERSE 7:

"Thou art all fair, my love; there is no spot in thee."

In verse 1 Jesus called us fair but here He goes further, using the word *all* before *fair*. He went over all the particulars (verses 2–6): our eyes, hair, teeth, lips, cheeks, neck, breasts, and fragrance. He pronounces us "all fair." He declares that there is no spot or blemish to ruin our beauty. He took care of every spot, dying in our place, that we could be new creatures, perfect creatures. How can He say that we are perfect? Let me offer another verse that reinforces this truth: "Thou art sanctified wholly in every part" (1 Thessalonians 5:23). We have been renewed. "If any man be in Christ, he is a new creature" (2 Corinthians 5:17). Because of Him, we have no imperfections. That's how He sees us. We need to see ourselves that way. Do you realize how the enemy holds us back by causing us to think we don't measure up? Here is my interpretation of verse 7.

KJV	MY VERSION
"Thou art all fair, my love; there is no spot in thee."	*"You are all fair, My love; you are beautiful all over. There is nothing imperfect in you."*

He delights in every aspect of who you are, of who I am. This amazes me. Of course, I realize that it is His work of redemption and sanctification that makes me "all fair." That fact just makes me love Him and praise Him even more. As you go back through to read my interpretation of this passage, know that Christ delights in the fragrance you release when you worship.

Reflections

If your prayers and worship could be described by a fragrance, what would the fragrance be, and why that particular fragrance?

_____

_____

_____

_____

To what degree do you believe that you are spotless?

Response

Love on Him. Let Him love on you. Record what He says to you.

WEEK FOUR

Song of Solomon 4:1–7

FAIR AND FRAGRANT

*H*oly Spirit impressed upon me that Song of Solomon 4 is about the bride or individual that has matured spiritually. "The bride has made herself ready" (Revelation 19:7). If a bride were getting ready for her wedding, she would apply eye shadow, eyeliner, and mascara. As a bride of Christ preparing for His return, we need to work on our eyes as well. According to Song of Solomon 4:1, we need to develop eyes that see as He sees, eyes that see in the realm of the spirit.

Verse 1 also mentions the hair. A bride would work a great deal on her hair to make sure it lays just right and then apply a covering of hairspray to guarantee that everything stays in place. A bride usually wears a veil over her head. As the bride of Christ, we are to embrace the glory of His covering.

Teeth are the subject of verse 2. A bride would certainly brush her teeth and make sure they look as good as possible. By chewing on the Word, we gain wisdom and develop balanced theology.

A bride would also apply lipstick. Verse 3 mentions crimson or blood-stained lips. Spiritually this happens when we speak the Word.

Learning to speak and agree with the Word is part of the maturing process, part of becoming ready for the bridegroom.

The bride would certainly apply rouge or some color to her cheeks. As the bride of Christ, we need to develop humility in our lives. Verse 3 shows how our humility pleases Him.

Hopefully, a bride has firmly made up her mind concerning this marriage she is about to enter. In that process, she has gotten to know very much about her intended. She has filled her mind with facts about him. No one could trick her with regards to his character. She knows him. Likewise, as verse 4 tells us, we need to fill our minds with truth from His word. Truths that will dismantle every lie of the enemy that comes against our relationship with our beloved Savior.

Verse 5 mentions breasts, which nurture the young. A young bride would certainly understand and prepare herself for the eventual birth and nursing of a child. As the bride of Christ, we need to develop the ability to teach and nurture those younger in the faith while always making sure our theology is balanced. We need to develop compassion and the ability to show mercy so that we can comfort those in need.

A bride preparing for her wedding should have already put aside all other lovers. She knows who satisfies her inner longings. We need to mature to the point that the world has no appeal to us. Verse 5 points out that we need to feed on Him and do so in the company of other believers.

I'm sure almost every bride wears a special perfume, one that she knows pleases her bridegroom. Verse 6 is where Jesus notices the fragrance released by our prayers and worship.

Lastly, a bride would be confident of where her lover retires each night. I'm reminded of Song of Solomon 1:13 where the bridegroom says He will lie between her breasts all night. Song of Solomon is such a passionate book, and this chapter, in particular, is very romantic. Jesus adores each one of us. Enjoy my rendition of Song of Solomon 4:1–7 with all the symbolism replaced. Hear Jesus saying these words to you:

"Look at yourself, My love, you are beautiful.
Really look now, you are beautiful.
Your eyes, under that veil, please Me
because you reserve them for My glances only.
Since you reserve them for Me only,
they see in the realm of the spirit.
I can show you great and mighty things that you know not of.
My glory upon you stunning.
You are extremely valuable to Me.
So valuable that all your hairs are numbered.
Oh yes, My beloved, you are clean and desirable;
and very beautiful.
You've carefully balanced your life with good theology;
You have washed your soul with My Word,
which has made you fruitful even to a double portion.
You are not spiritually barren.
Your lips are beautifully stained with My blood.
This is evident in your wise declarations of life.
I see your humility and modesty.
Oh, how you please Me.
Your lovely neck supports your mind,
which you have stocked piled as an armory
with weapons comparable to David's armory.
It contains a thousand truths from My word,
which become shields,
like the ones that belonged to David's mighty men.
You beautifully demonstrate comfort, mercy, and compassion.
With wisdom, you feed, nurture, and sustain
those younger than yourself.
You nourish yourself by feeding on Me and My body of believers.
I am very pleased with your fragrance, My beloved;

I delight in your worship and prayers.
I choose your heart of worship as My resting place and My abode.
You are all fair, My love; you are beautiful all over.
There is nothing imperfect in you."

Reflection and Response

I hope you are as touched by those words as I am. You are loved and considered very beautiful by your Savior. If you are doing this as a group Bible study, use day five as the day you come together. Go over the refection questions from each day together. Share, encourage, and pray for one another.

_____

_____

_____

If you are doing this study on your own, review the reflection and response sections from each day. Worship Him and ask Him to do a deeper work. Ask Him to add another layer of truth and beauty to your heart. Afterward, record your experience with Him here.

_____

_____

_____

WEEK FIVE

Song of Solomon 4:8

A DATE WITH JESUS

We're only going to cover one verse today, but it's packed with good stuff. I love studying the Song of Solomon. It helps me realize just how much He loves me. As you read verse 8, notice that He still wants us to look at something, just as He did since the beginning of the chapter. At first He wanted us to look at ourselves. Now the focus changes to something else. Let's dive in.

VERSE 8:
"Come with me from Lebanon, my spouse, with me from Lebanon: look from the top of Amana, from the top of Shenir and Hermon, from the lions' dens, from the mountains of the leopards."

Christ wants us to go with Him. He wants to take us somewhere, perhaps on a date. Cool. Or rather, He wants to take us away from somewhere, away "from Lebanon." Lebanon is a snow-covered mountain (Strong), which symbolizes the salvation experience. "Though your sins be as scarlet, they shall be white as snow" (Isaiah 1:18). Our salvation experience was certainly a spiritual mountain or high point in our life. Deuteronomy 3:25 calls Lebanon a "goodly mountain." I think we all agree that the salvation experience is beyond good. Hosea 14:6 says Lebanon has a "goodly smell" as does our salvation. Isaiah 35:2 refers to the "glory of Lebanon." Salvation is certainly glorious experience. However, the Word of God says we are to go from "glory to glory" (2 Corinthians 3:18). So, Christ calls us from Lebanon.

He wants to take us to Amana, which is a river. Amana River flows down from the top of a mountain with twin peaks: Shenir and Hermon (Henry). I believe this river is symbolic of the baptism in the Holy Spirit. Jesus wants us to press beyond salvation and experience the baptism of the Holy Spirit.

"Whoever believes in me, as Scripture has said, rivers of living water will flow from within them. By this, he meant the Spirit, whom those who believed in him were later to receive. Up to that time the Spirit had not been given, since Jesus had not yet been glorified" (John 7:38–39 NIV).

This twin-peaked mountain was also snow-covered (Henry). Again, snow refers to the cleansing work of Christ in our lives. To me, this signifies and reinforces the verse above (John 7:38–39). Jesus must be glorified in our lives before we can receive the baptism of the Holy Spirit. From the top of Mount Hermon, the Israelites could see the promised land (Henry). Holy Spirit is the One that gives us glimpses into our future and the wonderful things that God has in store for us. Jesus said, "Look!" He calls us forward from salvation into the baptism of the Spirit and He says, "Look! Look at all I have in store for you." Look at the promise land. Psalm 89:12 refers to the "joy of Hermon." It is truly joyful when we have the realization of what God has in store for us. Purpose! Destiny! Victory! Psalm 133:3 speaks of the "pleasant dew of Hermon." I would say that Holy Spirit and His plans for us are like a pleasant dew.

What about the other peak, the one called Shenir? If you look in one direction from Hermon, you could see the promise land. I like that view! Looking in the other direction from Shenir, the Israelites could see the desert land from which they came (Henry). Holy Spirit helps you see your past and your future, all of it snow-covered or under the blood of Jesus. That touches me. My past and my future are both snow-covered!

The verse goes on to say, "[Look] from the lion's dens, from the mountains of the leopards." The lion is symbolic of our enemy (Psalm 7:2; 1 Peter 5:8). Holy Spirit helps us see our enemy and his strategies against us when he is still far off.

Christ desires to lead His bride away from their past and the world into the high places of spiritual delight and victory. Now I present my interpretation of this wonderful verse:

KJV	MY VERSION
"Come with me from Lebanon, my spouse, with me from Lebanon: look from the top of Amana, from the top of Shenir and Hermon, from the lions' dens, from the mountains of the leopards."	*"Come with Me; My beloved. I have much in store for you. Come from your glorious salvation experience, which has made you white as snow. I have another mountain top for you. From this mountain flows the river of living water. Drink freely, deep deeply of My presence and My glory. Be filled to overflowing with My Holy Spirit. You will never thirst again. And come, yes, come over here to this mountain. From here you can see your future. Stand here at this altitude and behold the plans that I have for you. I have great things in store for you, My beloved. I know that you can see the lion lurking on the path that you must take. Come with Me, do not be afraid, My beloved bride. Come with Me. I'll go with you on this journey even through the valley of the shadow of death. I'll be with you, so do not fear. Come with Me."*

Read my rendition once again. It is packed with good stuff! Don't you love it? Jesus is speaking. He has places to take us and things to show us. That's why it's important to develop eyes that see in the realm of the spirit. Jesus says, "Look." If He tells us to do it, we need to step out in faith and look. *Looking* and actually *seeing* become much easier with the baptism of the Holy Spirit. Please don't be afraid to pursue the baptism of the Holy Spirit. If you want further reading regarding Holy Spirit baptism, start with reading the entire book of Acts. Notice that believers received this baptism after their salvation experience. Notice that it is distinct from water baptism.

Reflections

Replace the following symbolism with what they represent:

Lebanon _____

Snow-covered _____

Amana _____

Tell what the Israelites could see when they looked from:

Mount Hermon _____

Mount Shenir _____

Has Jesus given you a glimpse of the plans that He has for you? Explain.

___

Response

Spend some time in worship. Press into His Presence. Describe what Jesus is showing you.

___

WEEK FIVE

Song of Solomon 4:9–11

PASSION

The verses we will study today paint a passionate picture: a ravished heart, an exposed neck, love better than wine, intoxicating lotions or fragrances, moist lips, and a tongue. Yikes! Let's find out what all this means.

VERSE 9:

"Thou hast ravished my heart, my sister, my spouse; thou hast ravished my heart with one of thine eyes, with one chain of thy neck."

I ravish His heart! I wonder what that means? These three words: "ravished my heart" are replaced in the Hebrew language with one word: "hearted." It would say, "Thou hast hearted me." This phrase means 3 things, according to *Strong's Concordance*:

(1) made my heart beat faster
(2) wounded my heart
(3) stolen my heart from its good senses

The Hebrew translation of *sister* is "my intimate beloved." If you think about it, "my sister, my spouse" are incompatible. It is only with Christ that we are both His sister and His spouse. This is another confirmation that this book is an allegory depicting Christ's love for us.

Spouse translates to "bride, one who completes me." Think about that. In some way, beyond our understanding, we complete Christ. We make His heart beat faster. We wound it when we reject Him. We steal His heart when we worship Him.

She did all this damage to His heart with one of her "eyes" and "one chain of her neck." I want us to think about the neck first. This refers to the long, slender part of your neck, made even longer in ancient Egypt by the wrapping of chains around it. Even though we are not ancient Egyptian women, our necks are elongated when we angle our heads upward so that our eyes can behold Him. "Fix your eyes upon Jesus, the author and finisher of your faith" (Hebrews 12:1–2). This position, our heads angled up exposing our neck, with our eyes focused on Him, is what ravishes His heart. Read my interpretation of verse 9:

KJV	MY VERSION
"Thou hast ravished my heart, my sister, my spouse; thou hast ravished my heart with one of thine eyes, with one chain of thy neck."	*"My heart is pounding faster and faster, you have wounded and stolen My heart, My intimate beloved, My bride. When you look at Me, when you stretch your neck upward to look at Me, with love, adoration, and worship in your eyes, you ravish My heart."*

VERSE 10:

"How fair is thy love, my sister, my spouse! How much better is thy love than wine! And the smell of thine ointments than all spices!"

Notice that you get three exclamation points. Verse 10 makes it clear to me that He is speaking here of our love expressed through worship. The smell or fragrance of our ointments refers to worship. In chapter 1, we learned that His love is better than wine. Now He says that our love satisfies Him more than wine. My interpretation of verse 10:

KJV	MY VERSION
"How fair is thy love, my sister, my spouse! how much better is thy love than wine! and the smell of thine ointments than all spices!"	*"Your love is perfect My intimate beloved, My bride! Your love is better and more intoxicating wine! The fragrance created by your worship is better than all other spices combined!"*

VERSE 11:

"Thy lips, O my spouse, drop as the honeycomb: honey and milk are under thy tongue; and the smell of thy garments is like the smell of Lebanon."

Honeycomb refers to the Word. Psalm 19:10 says that His Word "is sweeter than honey and the honeycomb." Lips that drip as the honeycomb would drip His Word. Honey is symbolic of wisdom. Wisdom drips from our lips when His Word comes forth from our mouths. "Pleasant words are as a honeycomb, sweet to the soul and health to the bones" (Proverbs 16:24). The result of pleasant words is healing for the body (bones) and the soul. This healing is for us as we speak the Word over ourselves, and it is for others as we speak the Word over them.

In the natural realm, honey and milk are pleasant, nurturing staples to our existence. Milk is for babies. Honey is for the mature. Honey is wisdom, which comes with maturity. Applying this verse spiritually signifies growing up and maturing. We progress from the milk of the Word to the wisdom of the Word.

Let's look at the last phrase of verse 11: "the smell of thy garments is as the smell of Lebanon." A garment is an article of clothing. Her clothes smelled like Lebanon, the snow-covered mountain that symbolizes the salvation experience. "Though your sins be as scarlet, they shall be whiter than snow" (Isaiah 1:18). This garment symbolizes the robe of righteousness that Christ put on you at the time of your salvation. You didn't try to dress yourself. As you matured, you did not become righteous in your own eyes. You still wear the righteousness He provided (Isaiah 61:10, Revelation 19:8). Here is my rendition of verse 11:

KJV	MY VERSION
"Thy lips, O my spouse, drop as the honeycomb: honey and milk are under thy tongue; and the smell of thy garments is like the smell of Lebanon."	*"Your lips are very beautiful, My bride. You have realized the power of your own words and you use your mouth appropriately. Your words are pleasant to Me, My beloved; and they bring you the good of the land. Those words take you into the destiny, My promises and the future that I have planned for you. Ah (breathing deeply), you smell fresh and clean just like you did at salvation. You're still wearing the garment that I gave you. You are beautiful! Look at yourself, My darling, My love. You are beautiful."*

As you reread the translated verses, realize these are very passionate expressions of Christ's love for His bride, for the church, and for you. Love is an action verb. We have great proof of His love in that He died for His bride, for the church, for you.

Reflections

What effect does your worship have on Him?

_____

_____

_____

To what extent do you use your words wisely?

_____

_____

_____

This whole chapter is about looking at yourself and seeing what He sees. To what extent are you beginning to believe that you are beautiful?

_____

_____

_____

Response

Worship Him. Adore Him. Ravish His heart with your worship. Let Him ravish your heart. Record your experience with Him here.

_____
_____
_____
_____
_____
_____
_____
_____
_____
_____
_____
_____
_____

WEEK FIVE

Song of Solomon 4:12–14

FRAGRANT WORSHIP

Christ, our bridegroom, is still speaking. He is describing what He sees when He looks at us. Expressing what He wants us to see and know about ourselves.

VERSE 12:
*"A garden enclosed is my sister, my spouse;
a spring shut up, a fountain sealed."*

The garden is symbolic of your spirit. Think about the Garden of Eden in Genesis. This was a place where Adam and Eve had intimate fellowship with God. They walked with Him in the cool of the day. It's in your spirit that you can have intimate fellowship with your Savior. The garden in verse 12 was *enclosed*. The Hebrew word means "bolted shut." This garden was bolted shut to the world. It was a place reserved for Him alone. He called the garden "a spring shut up, a fountain sealed." Both of these terms refer to the well of living water within your spirit (John 4:14; John 7:38).

KJV	MY VERSION
"A garden enclosed is my sister, my spouse; a spring shut up, a fountain sealed."	*"Your spirit, My spouse, is a place of intimate fellowship with Me. Inside you, Holy Spirit, is a well of living water. The world is locked out."*

VERSE 13:

"*Thy plants are an orchard of pomegranates, with pleasant fruits; camphire, with spikenard.*"

Plants are growing in your garden, or spirit. The Bible says that we are to "abide in the vine" (John 15:4) and produce the "fruit of the spirit" (Galatians 5:22–23). It takes a lot of fruit to make an orchard. The Hebrew word for orchard means "a preserve or refuge," like a national park. Your spirit is like the Garden of Eden, where the Lord God made to grow every tree that is pleasant to the sight and good for food. Your spirit is a place where Jesus can walk and talk with you like God walked with Adam and Eve in the Garden of Eden.

The specific fruit mentioned is pomegranates, a sensual fruit that you would feed a lover (Henry). Jesus is saying that we are His lovers, and He is enjoying our fruit. Esther 2:12 tells us camphire and spikenard are spices that were used to prepare a concubine for the king. Before a concubine could go to the king's chamber, she had to complete twelve months of preparation. She went through six months of bathing with the oil of myrrh, then another six months bathing with perfumes that prepared her for the king's pleasure. In this verse, Jesus is telling us that we have been fitly prepared for His pleasure.

Camphire was a costly spice, and it signifies the price (or value) of a life. The Hebrew word means "ransom." It was also called *henna*, which means "emotional tenderness." Spikenard is a perfume applied as an ointment or cream. It symbolizes intimacy, extravagant worship, passionate worship, and "the fire of love" (Henry). Read my interpretation of verse 13:

KJV	MY VERSION
"Thy plants are an orchard of pomegranates, with pleasant fruits; camphire, with spikenard."	*"Yes, your spirit is like the Garden of Eden, full of plants and trees, that arouse My love for you. Your fruit is excellent and most pleasant to Me."*

<u>**VERSE 14:**</u>

"Spikenard and saffron; calamus and cinnamon, with all trees of frankincense; myrrh and aloes, with all the chief spices."

It's interesting that "spikenard" is in both verses 13 and 14. Its meaning is the same. So, we have a double portion of this perfumed ointment or cream, which symbolizes extravagant worship, passionate worship, and the fire of love or intimacy. We can never worship too much. Moreover, we should never question His desire for intimacy with us.

Saffron is an iridaceous plant with a distinct fragrance and flavor. Iridaceous means "having colors like a rainbow." This plant is very colorful, featuring a range of oranges and yellows. Rainbows symbolize God's promises, as in the story of Noah's Ark, when God put the rainbow in the sky as a promise that He would never again flood the whole earth. If you have this plant in your garden or spirit, then you've been soaking in His promises to the degree that now you smell like the promises themselves. I like that. I smell like His promises.

Calamus is a hollow, sweet stalk used for two purposes: a writing instrument and a pipe. As a writing instrument, ink would flow through the stalk. As a pipe, smoke would flow through it. We are to become so saturated with Him that He (His spirit) flows through us. This stalk was also used as a flagpole. We resemble a flagpole when we lift Him high in worship, displaying His goodness and virtues.

Cinnamon is a costly spice with restorative qualities. The fact that we are costly and valuable was proved when Christ paid His life for us. When we soak in that truth, we become filled with restorative qualities or resurrection life. Wow!

Frankincense is a spice that symbolizes holiness, sacrifice, and intercession. *Myrrh* is a spice used to prepare a dead body (Henry). This symbolizes embracing death to self and death to our flesh.

Aloe is a costly spice that symbolizes worship that costs us something (Henry). It's easy to worship when all is going well, but to worship when things are less than wonderful is a sacrifice of praise that is pleasing to Him.

These are the "chief spices," or the finest, most important spices. They are pleasant, strong aromatics that diffuse sweet fragrances. Below is my presentation of verse 14:

KJV	MY VERSION
"Spikenard and saffron; calamus and cinnamon, with all trees of frankincense; myrrh and aloes, with all the chief spices."	*"My senses are aroused at your emotional tenderness. Oh, that extravagant, passionate worship! It produces a fragrance that lures Me into intimacy with you. Your beauty is like a rainbow, My love. It's obvious you have been soaking in My promises. You have purified and prepared yourself for My glory. Beloved, I am aware of your sacrifices and what I have cost you. You have died to yourself. Oh, the fragrance of your holiness, the aroma of your worship, the sincerity of your intercession; You move Me deeply! Ah, such a sweet fragrance. You have become so saturated with Me that I am flowing through you. Beloved, you are altogether pleasant to Me, valuable and of great use."*

As you go back and reread my rendition of these verses, realize that passionate worship ravishes His heart.

Reflections

As a result of this study, to what degree do you find yourself stepping into greater intimacy with Jesus?

_____

_____

_____

What does it mean to soak in His promises? To smell like His promises?

_____

_____

_____

Write out John 4:23.

_____

_____

_____

What does this verse mean to you?

_____

_____

_____

Response

Invite Him into a time of intimacy. Worship Him. Linger with Him. Adore Him. Thank Him for His promises. Afterward, record your time with Him here. Did He say anything to your spirit? Did He show you anything?

_____

_____

_____

_____

_____

_____

_____

_____

_____

_____

_____

_____

WEEK FIVE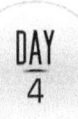

Song of Solomon 4:15

YOUR SPIRIT

We are only going to cover one verse today. My prayer is that at the end of this lesson, we all have a deeper understanding of our human spirit, the Holy Spirit within it, and what it is to worship Him in spirit and truth.

VERSE 15:
"A fountain of gardens, a well of living waters, and streams from Lebanon."

The fountain, well, and streams all speak of the Holy Spirit moving and living within our spirit (John 4:14). Just as the Garden of Eden was a place where Adam and Eve walked with the Lord, your spirit is to be a place of intimacy for you and the Lord. The Garden of Eden had a river flowing through it, and so do you. It is the river of the Holy Spirit. *Living waters* are waters that are alive and fresh. The water of the Holy Spirit is alive and fresh, never stagnant. The Hebrew meaning of *streams* is "to flow, to trickle, or to drip." I want to dig out some truths about the river within our spirit based on the river that flowed through the Garden of Eden. Genesis 2:8–15 is our text:

> "And the Lord God planted a garden eastward in Eden; and there he put the man whom he had formed . . . And a river went out of Eden to water the garden; and from thence it was parted and became into four heads. The name of the first is Pison: that is it which compasseth the whole land of Havilah, where there is gold; And the gold of that land is good: there is bdellium and the onyx stone. And the name of the second river is Gihon: the same is it that compasseth the whole land of Ethiopia. And the name of the third river is Hiddekel: that is it which goeth toward the east of Assyria. And the fourth river is Euphrates. And the Lord God took the man and put him into the garden of Eden to dress it and to keep it."

The Garden of Eden had four rivers flowing out of the main river. As we study these rivers, keep in mind that we are drawing a parallel to the river that flows through your spirit and waters your garden. The first river is Pison, which means "disperse broadly." Whatever is in your spirit will flow out and affect the atmosphere and those around you. If your spirit is full of fear, worry, pride, arrogance, anger, or bitterness, then that's what you release to those around you. Likewise, if your spirit is full of joy or peace, then that's what you release to those around you. Pison affected the whole land of Havilah, which means "circular," like a whirlpool. The attributes that most describe you circle around you, completely taking over your character. Pison also flows where there is gold. Gold is purified by fire. Likewise, trials have a way of dealing with and ridding us of those undesirable characteristics and replacing them with the good ones. This first river flows where there is bdellium, which means "pearls." A pearl is formed after enduring much pressure and agitation inside the shell. Pison also flows where there is onyx, a green gemstone that symbolizes eternal life. Gold is mentioned again in connection with this first river to show its purpose is to purify us. The Holy Spirit performs a continual purifying work in our lives. John said that Jesus would baptize us with the "Holy Ghost and with fire." Our spirits, our garden, must be purified by the fire of the Holy Spirit.

The second river is Gihon, which means "a stream that gushes forth and labors to break forth." This river stretches around Ethiopia, which is symbolic of the world. The Holy Spirit flows powerfully through our lives, enabling us to break through all our worldly struggles.

Hiddekel is the name of the third river. It means "rapid river." Today this river is called the Tigris, and it is still a rapidly moving river. This signifies that once breakthrough is made with regards to our purification and breaking free of worldly strongholds, we begin to make rapid and marked progress as a Christian.

The fourth and last river is the Euphrates, which means "fruitful, increase, prosperity, floods of plenty, and more than enough." With the Holy Spirit flowing freely through us, we become fruitful for His kingdom. We increase His territory and ours. We experience prosperity, plenty, and more than enough.

This is the adventure that the Holy Spirit takes us on. It is a progressive work. First is Pison; this is the refining process where our character traits, which are contrary to the fruit of the Spirit as described in Galatians 5, are dealt with by the mighty river of the Holy Spirit flowing within us. Second is Gihon; this is our season of breakthrough from our struggles with worldliness. It is the power of the river of God within us that causes us to break through into a place of personal victory. Third is Hiddekel; this is where we begin to make rapid progress as a victorious Christian. And fourth is Euphrates; here we finally become fruitful for His Kingdom and experience personal prosperity.

I love that these rivers from the Garden of Eden represent the work of the Holy Spirit in our lives, flowing through us, making our spirits (gardens) fruitful and pleasant. Here's my translation of verse 15:

KJV	MY VERSION
"A fountain of gardens, a well of living waters, and streams from Lebanon."	*"You welcomed the work of My Holy Spirit in your spirit. You allowed the Holy Spirit to refine you; Enabling you to break free of worldly snares; Because of this, you have made rapid spiritual progress, and have become very fruitful, impacting everyone around you. My fresh and living water is flowing through you. Beloved, you are like a stream releasing My saving grace into the world. I take great pleasure in you, My bride."*

Let's review "streams of Lebanon." In verse 8 we learned that Lebanon was a white, snow-covered mountain that symbolizes the salvation experience. Salvation is also the result of the Holy Spirit drawing us to Jesus. When you reread verse 15, know that Jesus is speaking these words over you.

Reflections

List two ways the Garden of Eden is like your spirit?

1. _____
   _____

2. _____
   _____

What do the four rivers in the Garden of Eden symbolize in your life?

Pison: _____
_____
_____

Gihon: _____
_____
_____

Hiddekel: _____
_____
_____

Euphrates: _____

_____

_____

Which of the four rivers describe the Holy Spirit's activity within you at this stage of your life?

_____

_____

_____

Response

Do you realize that the Holy Spirit is the third person of the Godhead and that you should worship Him too? Worship the Holy Spirit, and thank Him for His refining work, for helping you break through worldly obstacles, for helping you become a victorious Christian, and for blessing you and making you fruitful. Afterward, record your encounter with Holy Spirit.

_____

_____

_____

_____

WEEK FIVE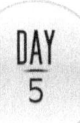

Song of Solomon 4:16

BLOW, SPIRIT . . . BLOW

Jesus has been speaking since verse 1, but the next verse is spoken by the Shulamite woman.

VERSE 16:
"Awake, O north wind; and come, thou south; Blow upon my garden, that the spices thereof may flow out. Let my beloved come into his garden, And eat his pleasant fruits."

The Hebrew meaning of *awake* means "rouse yourself." The bride calls for the wind to awaken or stir itself up. She calls for the south wind, which is symbolic of adversity. The reason I believe the south wind signifies adversity is because when you look at a map, south is at the bottom. We point up to indicate heaven and down to indicate hell, or the bottomless pit. She welcomes adversity because of the purifying effect it would have on her life. She wanted to please only her bridegroom and, therefore, embraced the refining process, even longed for it. She called for the north wind. On a map, north is on top, in the upper section. The north wind would be from heaven, the wind of the Holy Spirit. Think of Acts 2 where the Holy Spirit took the form of a rushing, mighty wind. In Acts, that wind filled the house. We need that wind to fill our house, our spirit. The bride calls for the wind to blow upon her garden, her spirit. The Hebrew word for blow means "breathe upon." Again, this is a picture of the Holy Spirit. The wind releases the spices or fragrance from the garden. The spices or fragrance represent our worship flowing out to God, and they also represent the fragrance of Christ flowing from us into the world. If the wind does not blow (if Holy Spirit does not move), the fragrance does not leave the garden.

Verse 16: "Let my beloved come into his garden And taste its choice fruits."

This is the bride inviting the bridegroom into her spirit, into intimacy. She has tended her garden so that its fruit will please Him. Likewise, we need to yield to the refining work of the Holy Spirit so that ours spirits please Christ. We need to invite Him into a deeper level of intimacy. Make this verse your prayer. Below is my interpretation of verse 16:

KJV	MY VERSION
"Awake, O north wind; and come, thou south; blow upon my garden, that the spices thereof may flow out. Let my beloved come into his garden, and eat his pleasant fruits."	"Wake up winds! Blow over me! Winds of adversity blow over my life, blow away that which does not please my Love. Holy Spirit blow over me and through me. Blow my praises out to my Beloved. Blow His fragrance from my spirit out into the world. Jesus, come into my spirit and partake of me."

I trust you can now appreciate why I broke the study of this chapter into two weeks. We have uncovered a huge amount of truth. Here's Song of Solomon 4, all sixteen verses. The symbolism has been replaced with words that we can apply to our relationship with Jesus. Remember that Christ is speaking for most of the chapter.

"Look at yourself, My love, you are beautiful.
Really look now, you are beautiful.
Your eyes, under that veil, please Me
because you reserve them for My glances only.
Since you reserve them for Me only,
they see in the realm of the spirit.
I can show you great and mighty things
that you know not of.
My glory upon you stunning.
You are extremely valuable to Me.
So valuable that all your hairs are numbered.
Oh yes, my beloved, you are clean,
desirable, and very beautiful.
You've carefully balanced your life with good theology;
You have washed your soul with My Word,
which has made you fruitful even to a double portion.
You are not spiritually barren.
Your lips are beautifully stained with My blood.
This is evident in your wise declarations of life.
I see your humility and modesty.
Oh, how you please Me.
Your lovely neck supports your mind,
which you have stocked piled as an armory
with weapons comparable to David's armory.
It contains a thousand truths from My word, which become shields,

like the ones that belonged to David's mighty men.
You beautifully demonstrate comfort, mercy, and compassion.
With wisdom, you feed, nurture and sustain those younger than yourself.
You nourish yourself by feeding on Me and My body of believers.
I am very pleased with your fragrance, My beloved;
I delight in your worship and prayers.
I choose your heart of worship as My resting place and My abode.
You are all fair, My love; you are beautiful all over.
There is nothing imperfect in you.
Come with Me; My beloved. I have much in store for you.
Come from your glorious salvation experience,
which has made you white as snow.
I have another mountain top for you.
From this mountain flows the river of living water.
Drink freely, deep deeply of My presence and My glory.
Be filled to overflowing with My Holy Spirit.
You will never thirst again.
And come, yes, come over here to this mountain.
From here you can see your future.
Stand here at this altitude and behold the plans that I have for you.
I have great things in store for you, My beloved.
I know that you can see the lion lurking on the path that you must take.
Come with Me, do not be afraid, My beloved bride. Come with Me.
I will go with you on this journey
even through the valley of the shadow of death.
I will be with you, so do not fear.
Come with Me.
You will inherit the land if you come.
My heart is pounding faster and faster,
You have wounded and stolen My heart,
My intimate beloved, My bride.

*Your neck in that position of worship
and your eyes fixed on adoring Me
is ravishing My heart!
I love your worship!
It's better than intoxicating wine.
It brings more pleasure to My senses
than the best smelling spices.
You ravish My heart!
Your lips are very beautiful, My spouse.
You have realized the power of your own words
and you use your mouth appropriately.
Your words are pleasant to Me, My beloved.
And those words bring you the good of the land;
those words take you into your destiny,
into My promises and the future that I have planned for you.
Ah (breathing deeply), you smell fresh and clean
just like you did at salvation.
You're still wearing the garment that I gave you.
You are beautiful! Look at yourself, My darling, My love.
You are beautiful.
Your spirit, My spouse, is a place of intimate fellowship with Me.
Inside you, Holy Spirit is a well of living water.
The world is locked out.
Yes, your spirit is like the Garden of Eden,
full of plants and trees which arouse My love for you.
Your fruit is excellent and most pleasant to Me.
My senses are aroused at your emotional tenderness.
Oh, that extravagant, passionate worship!
It produces a fragrance that lures Me into intimacy with you.
Your beauty is like the rainbow, My love.
It's obvious you have been soaking in My promises.*

You have purified and prepared yourself for My glory.
Beloved, I am aware of your sacrifices and what I have cost you.
You have died to yourself.
Oh, the fragrance of your holiness, the aroma of your worship,
the sincerity of your intercession;
You move Me deeply!
Ah, such a sweet fragrance.
You have become so saturated with Me that I am flowing through you.
Beloved, you are altogether pleasant to Me, valuable and of great use.
You welcomed the work of My Holy Spirit in your spirit.
You allowed Holy Spirit to refine you.
Enabling you to break free of worldly snares.
Because of this, you have made rapid spiritual progress,
and have become very fruitful, impacting everyone around you.
My fresh and living water is flowing through you.
Beloved, you are like a stream releasing
My saving grace into the world.
I take great pleasure in you, My bride.
Wake up winds! Blow over me!
Winds of adversity blow over my life,
Blow away that which does not please my Love.
Holy Spirit blow over me and through me.
Blow my praises out to my Beloved.
Blow His fragrance from my spirit out into the world.
Jesus, come into my spirit and partake of me."

Reflection and Response

In the first fifteen verses, the bridegroom (Christ) extends an invitation for deeper intimacy. Recall the Shulamite woman's response in verse 16. In your own words, respond to Jesus, the lover of your soul. Be sincere. Invite Him into your garden, your spirit. Get alone with Him. Know and experience His love. If you have not yet received the infilling of the Holy Spirit, continue to seek Him for it. Record your thoughts.

_____

_____

_____

_____

_____

If you are doing this as a group Bible study, use day five as the day you come together. Go over the refection questions from each day together. Share, encourage, and pray for one another.

_____

_____

_____

_____

_____

WEEK SIX

Song of Solomon 5:1

AN INTIMATE DINNER

To fully appreciate chapter 5, we must refresh our memory of the last verse we read, 4:16:

"Awake, O north wind; and come, thou south; blow upon my garden, that the spices thereof may flow out. Let my beloved come into his garden, and eat His pleasant fruits."

The bride called for the north wind or the wind of the Holy Spirit to blow over her. This will release her fragrance and lure Jesus into her garden, which symbolizes her spirit. She has tended her garden and allowed the Holy Spirit to work in it so that her fruit will please Him. She so desperately wants Him that she even calls for winds of adversity to refine her spirit and draw Him into it.

In chapter 5:1, Jesus responds to the fragrance released from her spirit. Jesus responds to the fragrance created by the Holy Spirit blowing over us. Jesus responds to the fragrance created by the winds of adversity blowing over us. The fragrance released is our worship. We should worship when we sense the winds of the Holy Spirit and also during the difficult times of adversity or trial. He responds to our worship, to our desire for Him. We need to stir up desire.

VERSE 1:
"I am come into my garden, my sister, my spouse: I have gathered my myrrh with my spice; I have eaten my honeycomb with my honey; I have drunk my wine with my milk: Eat, O friends, drink, yea, drink abundantly, O beloved."

How does He respond? By coming into her garden, her spirit. Notice that He calls the garden "my garden." He does not say, "I have come into your garden," but "my garden." We must fully surrender our spirit so that it is His.

He addresses her as "my sister," which means "my beloved one who is part of me." It is hard to understand, but just as a man and his wife become one when they consummate their love, we become part of Christ when we yield to His love. He also calls her "my spouse," which means my bride and comes from a root word meaning "to complete, perfect, make complete, or make perfect." It is way beyond my understanding, but in some way, we complete Jesus. He doesn't need us; however, He desires us and loves us so deeply that our acceptance of His love completes Him. This blows me away!

Notice that He gathers "His" myrrh and "His" spice. The things in our garden become His. Myrrh is a sacred oil that was burned daily as incense in the temple. Incense is symbolic of our prayers and worship. He gathers our worship to Himself. Our worship belongs to Him and only Him.

He eats things that are not normally found in a garden: honeycomb, honey, wine, and milk. There are two trains of thought regarding this. First, it is possible that He ate the fruit of the garden and also brought honeycomb, honey, wine, and milk (which are products of the promise land) into the garden. Another thought is that perhaps the honeycomb, honey, wine, and milk were prepared by the bride just like Esther prepared a banquet of wine for her husband, the king. We will not rule out either one of those because it is not clear.

Consider this line: "Eat, O friends; drink, yea, drink abundantly, O beloved." It reveals that Jesus did bring the extra items. Jesus invites His friends and His beloved (that's us) to eat. This makes me think He provided the additional items.

So, let's go with the thought that Christ provided the honeycomb, honey, wine, and milk. The word *honeycomb* can be found in Psalm 19:10, which says that His law, judgments, or Word "is sweeter than honey and the honeycomb." He is inviting us to eat His Word (Matthew 4:4).

Honey is symbolic of wisdom and revelation. It is a truth from the Word revealed or made real to you by the Holy Spirit. This comes by prayerfully meditating on the Word. Honeycomb has to be chewed and chewed to get the rich flavor out. When we prayerfully meditate on the Word, it becomes wisdom and revelation to us. In the spiritual realm, the young in Christ drink the milk of the Word while the mature eat the wisdom of the Word (Hebrews 5:12–14).

The truly mature drink wine. We learned in an earlier chapter that wine makes the heart glad or joyful. Christ wants us full of true joy, which only comes from partaking of Him (John 15:11). Wine is symbolic of the Holy Spirit (Ephesians 5:18) and of the Lord healing us (1 Timothy 5:23; Luke 10:34). Wine is also symbolic of blood. The wine used in communion represents the blood of Jesus (1 Corinthians 11:25).

Verse 1 begins with Jesus coming into her spirit and enjoying the worship, the worship that is His. He then speaks to His friends and His beloved. That's the bride as a whole and us as individuals. John 15:15 says that we are friends of Jesus. He invites us to partake of Him. He offers us honeycomb: His Word. He offers us honey: wisdom and revelation from His Word. He offers us milk, which helps us grow and mature. He offers us wine, which symbolizes the Holy Spirit, joy, healing, and the complete work of His blood. Wow! My rendition of verse 1 is as follows:

KJV	MY VERSION
"I am come into my garden, my sister, my spouse: I have gathered my myrrh with my spice; I have eaten my honeycomb with my honey; I have drunk my wine with my milk: eat, O friends; drink, yea, drink abundantly, O beloved."	*"I have entered My garden; your spirit has become My garden. My beloved, you are part of Me. My bride, you are the one who completes Me and makes Me whole. I have gathered your prayers and your worship; they are a sweet fragrance to Me. O friends, O beloved, come eat with Me, I bring My Word to the table, it tastes like honeycomb. The honey becomes wisdom in your mouth. Drink, yes, drink deeply of all that I have for you. Drink milk, and when it no longer satisfies you, Drink of the wine of My spirit. Drink deeply. Drink and be filled with joy. Drink and be healed. Drink of all that I make available to you. Drink deeply until you are intoxicated with My love."*

As you reread the translated version of verse 5:1, remember that this verse goes with 4:16, where she invites Him into the garden to partake of her. These two verses indicate intimacy between the bridegroom and the bride. They indicate a partaking of each other. He says to "Drink, drink abundantly." *Strong's Concordance* says to "drink abundantly" means drink until "intoxicated" with His love. I like that— intoxicated by love.

Reflections

Jesus calls you His sister. What does that mean?

_____

_____

_____

_____

_____

Jesus calls you His spouse. What does that mean?

_____

_____

_____

_____

Response

Worship Him. Invite Him into your spirit to partake of you. He will (no doubt) show up and bless your heart—perhaps with honey, honeycomb, milk, or even wine. Afterward, record the encounter here.

_____
_____
_____
_____
_____
_____
_____
_____
_____
_____
_____
_____
_____
_____

WEEK SIX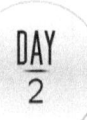

Song of Solomon 5:2–6

AWAKEN TO HIS CALL

I trust that you enjoyed the romantic dinner you shared with Jesus at the end of yesterday's lesson. Unfortunately, in today's lesson, we find the bride alone, totally separated from the bridegroom. What happened to destroy their intimacy? Let's find out.

VERSE 2:
"I sleep, but my heart waketh: it is the voice of my beloved that knocketh, saying, Open to me, my sister, my love, my dove, my undefiled: for my head is filled with dew, and my locks with the drops of the night."

The scene changes from the romantic garden dinner to a bedroom scene. The bride is alone. She is asleep. Sleep comes from a root word, which means "negligent, lethargic, stale, or dead." The bride is spiritually sleeping. Her spirit is not alert. Perhaps through neglect, her spirit has become stale and lethargic.

Scripture warns us that no one knows when the bridegroom will appear and that he will find some sleeping (Mark 13:32–37). I am reminded of the ten virgins (Matthew 25:5, 13). While they slept, He came. Even when we are physically asleep, we must learn to keep our spirit alert and sharp. I practice prayer before sleep, committing my dreams to Him and praying in the spirit while falling asleep. Many times, I wake up praying in the spirit. Often, I have spiritual dreams. I almost always wake with a song of praise coming from my spirit.

The bride hears His voice, and it wakes her. Her heart wakes up. *Heart* refers to the inner man or the spirit of man. Her spirit heard the voice of the bridegroom. We need to cultivate a spirit that hears and knows His voice even when we are asleep. *Wake* comes from a root word, meaning "to be exposed or laid bare." For her to say, "My heart wakes" would be like saying, "My heart is laid bare. It is exposed."

The voice of her beloved knocks. "Knock" is also found in Revelation 3:20: "Behold, I stand at the door and knock." He knocks to awaken us so that we would let Him in. How does He knock? By His Word and by His Spirit. He knocks by afflictions, large or small situations that cause us to think of needing His help. He knocks by blessings, those things that cause our hearts to murmur our thanks to Him. Note that He is a gentleman. He does not force Himself on us. He knocks.

He asks her to open the door of her heart or spirit. He calls her "my love," which means "my intimate friend." He then calls her "my dove," which indicates "my mate forever." This points to the fact that doves mate for life. Dove comes from a root word that means "wine or effervesce." This is another truth that blows me away. Wine is mentioned several times throughout Song of Solomon as pointing to His love for us. His love makes our hearts glad and light. Twice in Song of Solomon He calls us doves (2:14, 5:2) or wine. We make His heart glad and light! Wine is symbolic of the Holy Spirit (Ephesians 5:18). With the word *effervesce* in mind, consider John 7:37–39 wherein Jesus said believers would have rivers of living water flowing out of their spirit due to the infilling of the Holy Spirit. Also consider Numbers 21:17, where Israel sang, "Spring up, oh well." When our worship is yielded to the Holy Spirit and comes from deep within our spirit, it flows up and out of us, almost effervescing and is like wine to Jesus. This kind of worship makes His heart light and glad. Again, this blows me away!

Before I leave the subject of doves, I want you to notice that I didn't go into this truth in Chapter 2, where it mentions turtledoves. That is because I did not uncover the truth until I studied the verse in chapter 4. Worshipfully read and study the Word right in His presence, call upon Him and He will show you great and mighty things that you did not know (Jeremiah 33:3). He will show you. You are His dove. You have dove's eyes.

He also calls us *undefiled*, which means "complete, perfect, pure ones." We are complete, perfect, and pure in Him. Note that Jesus does not scold her for sleeping rather than waiting up for Him, but instead He calls out to her in the kindest most endearing ways imaginable: "My sister, My love, My dove, My undefiled." He expresses His tender affection to her. His love is unconditional. He admonishes her to open the door because His head is filled with dew and His locks with drops of the night. His head was covered with a night mist or dew. His hair was dripping wet with it. Commentaries suggest this represents the hardships Jesus has gone through for us. The crown of thorns would have caused His head and hair to be wet, dripping with blood. He wanted her to consider what He went through for her. My interpretation of this overwhelming verse follows:

KJV	MY VERSION
"I sleep, but my heart waketh: it is the voice of my beloved that knocketh, saying, Open to me, my sister, my love, my dove, my undefiled: for my head is filled with dew, and my locks with the drops of the night."	"I am indulging in sleep, my spirit is at ease and comfortable, but suddenly my spirit wakes up. Whose voice is that? It is the voice of my Beloved. My heart is exposed, my slumber and negligence are obvious. He is knocking on my heart; He is calling for me. *Open your spirit, My beloved, you are part of Me. Open your spirit, My love, My intimate friend. Open your spirit, My dove, My only mate forever. You make My heart glad and light. Open your spirit, My undefiled, My perfect bride; For I am overwhelmed with desire for you. Consider the hardships I have endured to be intimate with you. Consider the blood that covered My head and dripped from My hair. Open your spirit, Let Me into your heart.*"

VERSE 3:

"I have put off my coat; how shall I put it on? I have washed my feet; how shall I defile them?"

Wow, talk about excuses. There is no hidden meaning in these words. *Coat* is a garment, robe, or covering. *Washed* literally means washed, and *feet* literally mean feet. *Defile* means "to soil." The commentaries were not extremely helpful here. After much prayer, the Holy Spirit impressed the following upon me: She is concerned about her coat or, in other words, her religion. She is concerned about the fact that through religious duty she has washed her feet, and now walking across the floor to Christ they will become defiled. In truth, He is the only way they will become clean. Instead of the coat of religion, we need to wear the robe of righteousness that He provides. It is a state of righteousness that does not depend on what we have or have not done. "He became sin, that we might become the righteousness of God in Him" (2 Corinthians 5:21). This is my rendition of verse 3:

KJV	MY VERSION
"I have put off my coat; how shall I put it on? I have washed my feet; how shall I defile them?"	"I cannot open to You because I have done my religious duties. I have washed my feet, if I come to You, they will be soiled."

VERSE 4:
"My beloved put in his hand by the hole of the door, and my bowels were moved for him."

Beloved means "my lover." *Hand* signifies His power or strength. *Hole* is a place of access. *Door* signifies the heart or spirit, the place where Christ enters into our lives. So, in our weakness or inability, He compassionately and powerfully touches our spirit enabling us to come to Him. When we feel that we cannot approach Him, we should ask for

His strength and grace. His gracious touch caused her bowels to move for Him. That sounds weird, and it's not romantic at all. *Bowels* signify the place of deep emotions, like compassion, distress, or love. Shockingly, *Strong's Concordance* says bowels refer to the organs of procreation, "the womb." *Moved* means "to moan like a soul in prayer."

Before I tell you what this verse is saying, let me remind you that our intimacy with Jesus is in the realm of the spirit. It is not a physical intimacy. She is saying that she is overwhelmed with the desire to be intimate and become impregnated by Him. Read on for my presentation of verse 4:

KJV	MY VERSION
"My beloved put in his hand by the hole of the door, and my bowels were moved for him."	"My lover powerfully touched my spirit with His grace. My womb moaned for Him. I was overwhelmed with desire to be intimate with Him and reproduce for Him."

VERSE 5:
"I rose up to open to my beloved; and my hands dropped with myrrh, and my fingers with sweet smelling myrrh, upon the handles of the lock."

Myrrh is oil that represents anointing, and it symbolizes our worship. However, in this case, the myrrh is from Him. It is the grace, or anointing, to do something. This anointing oil was on the door and the lock of the door. The door is where we allow Him access into our lives. The lock would be our walls of self-protection. He gave her the grace to let down her walls and to open the door to Him. We really cannot take any credit for having Him in our lives. All we can take credit for is rejecting Him or turning Him away. Read below for my interpretation of verse 5:

KJV	MY VERSION
"I rose up to open to my beloved; and my hands dropped with myrrh, and my fingers with sweet smelling myrrh, upon the handles of the lock."	"I rose to open my spirit to my Love. I touched the lock and my hands dripped with grace to open the door. My fingers were covered with His sweet-smelling fragrance."

VERSE 6:
"I opened to my beloved; but my beloved had withdrawn himself, and was gone: my soul failed when he spake: I sought him, but I could not find him; I called him, but he gave me no answer."

That first line is clear enough. When she opened the door of her spirit to let Him in, He was gone. *Withdrawn* means He turned away. *Soul* is different from the spirit of man. The soul is the mind, will, and emotions. She knew immediately that her soul had failed her. Her reasoning, her will, or perhaps an emotional condition of her heart kept her from opening the door when He first spoke. Hebrews 3:15 says there is an accepted time, a day to hear His voice or call. When the acceptable time is gone, it's gone. Who determines the time? He does (Psalm 32:6; Isaiah 49:8; Genesis 6:3).

Henry wrote that "my soul failed" was her reaction when she saw He had turned away. She became distraught. There was mental anguish and emotional upheaval. I'm reminded of the New Testament account of the man beside the Pool of Bethesda. When the water stirs, get in. Do not wait and miss the opportunity.

The second part of verse 6 has her searching for Him but not finding Him. We search for Him by worship and prayer and in His Word. He did not answer or respond. Notice that she did not give up and go back to bed. She went in pursuit of Him.

We are to seek with effort. Do not give in to complacency. Complacency leads to a spiritual drought, which is not good for a garden (Psalm 63:1). My interpretation of verse 6 can hopefully bring clearer understanding:

KJV	MY VERSION
"I opened to my beloved; but my beloved had withdrawn himself, and was gone: my soul failed when he spake: I sought him, but I could not find him; I called him, but he gave me no answer."	"I opened to my Beloved; but my Beloved had withdrawn Himself, and was gone: Oh, why did I fail to respond when He called to me? I sought Him with worship and prayer, but I could not find Him; I had no sense of His favor, of His comfort, of His love. I was thoroughly distraught. I cried out to Him in worship and prayer, I begged, but He did not answer me."

I cannot imagine making all that effort and Jesus not responding. I think about the verse from John that says, "Draw near to God, and He will draw near to you." The trouble is that we forget the rest of that verse, which describes what it means to draw near: "Cleanse your hands, you sinners; and purify your hearts, you double-minded" (James 4:8).

Tomorrow's lesson will reveal why Jesus did not respond to her efforts to draw Him back. Please go back and reread my presentation of verses 2–6.

Reflections

Can you think of a time that you experienced being physically asleep but still alert spiritually? If so, please describe the experience.

_____

_____

_____

How can religion and religious works hinder our relationship with Jesus?

_____

_____

_____

To what degree do you believe Jesus desires fellowship with you?

_____

_____

_____

Response

Worship and spend some time with Jesus. Ask Him to reveal any religious mind-sets or habits you may be holding on to. Afterward, record your encounter with Him.

WEEK SIX

Song of Solomon 5:7–8

WATCHMEN THAT DESTROY

The bride was already distraught because Jesus was nowhere to be found. Now things appear to be getting even worse for her. Let's see what we can learn from this passage.

VERSE 7:
"The watchmen that went about the city found me. They smote me, they wounded me; The keepers of the walls took away my veil from me."

This verse sounds violent. Watchmen are keepers or guards that have charge of something or someone. A city has watchmen that keep it or guard over it. A city has principalities and powers assigned to it, both demonic and angelic powers that guard and influence the city. The watchmen in this verse were no doubt demonic. You are probably aware that the heavenly Father has assigned a guardian angel to watch over you. You may not be aware that satan has assigned a demon to you. This demon's job is to watch for an opportunity to steal, kill, and destroy (John 10:10). It watches for any vulnerability. These demons *smote* her, which means "hit, struck, beat, and tortured" her. They *wounded* her, which means "split, bruised, crushed." They did this violence to her spirit. They bruised it, crushed it, and wounded it. When she said they "took away my veil," she meant they exposed her humanity, her vulnerability. It means they shamed her. I'm aware that many of us have experienced feelings of shame. It is helpful to realize that the source of those feelings is demonic. Here is my explanation of verse 7:

KJV	MY VERSION
"The watchmen that went about the city found me, they smote me, they wounded me; the keepers of the walls took away my veil from me."	"The evil principalities and powers that are assigned to my destruction found me. They attacked me, they hit me, they beat me, they tortured me. They wounded, bruised and crushed my spirit. Those evil principalities who watch for the vulnerable, they violently exposed me and shamed me."

VERSE 8:
"I charge you, O daughters of Jerusalem if ye find my beloved, that ye tell him, that I am sick of love."

In chapter 3 we learned that the *daughters* refers to those who build or rebuild a family by giving birth. *Jerusalem* is a city in Palestine that consists of two hills. The names of the hills mean "rare" and "peace." So, *daughters of Jerusalem* would mean "rare daughters of peace."

The word *sick* means "to be weakened or sickened because of grief or sorrow." To be sick of love would indicate being lovesick. My rendering of verse 8:

KJV	MY VERSION
"I charge you, O daughters of Jerusalem, if ye find my beloved, that ye tell him, that I am sick of love."	"I charge you, rare daughters of peace, who rebuild and restore, If you find my Love, tell Him that I am grieved, and sorry. Tell Him His absence has left me weak and helpless, Tell Him that I am lovesick for Him."

Please go back and reread my presentation of verses 7 and 8 together. This is a very sad picture. The bride is alone and abused, sorrowfully and humbly seeking restoration with the lover of her soul.

Reflections

Do you now or have you ever struggled with shame? If your answer is yes, please write about your experience with shame.

_____

_____

_____

What is the source of these feelings?

_____

_____

What does Ephesians 1:6 have to say about you?

Response

Worship Jesus. Press into His love and let Him minister to you in any area of shame. Let Him cover that area with His blood. Let Him bring healing and restoration to your heart. Afterward, record your encounter with Him here.

WEEK SIX

Song of Solomon 5:9–16

A METAPHORICAL DESCRIPTION OF JESUS

I titled this A Metaphorical Description of Jesus, and it is certainly that. It will bless you as we uncover all the symbolism about our Savior, our Jesus. Some of it is quite shocking, so get ready to be overwhelmed by His heart for you.

We ended yesterday with verse 8, where the bride asked the daughters of Jerusalem to tell Jesus that she desperately wanted to be reconciled to Him. In verse 9 they respond to her with a question about her beloved.

VERSE 9:
"What is thy beloved more than another beloved, O thou fairest among women? What is thy beloved more than another beloved, that thou dost so charge us?"

Notice the respectful title the daughters of Jerusalem give to the spouse: "O thou fairest among women!" We learned earlier that fairest means most beautiful. They saw spectacular beauty in her, which was due to His grace in her life. The word *women* refers to married women. They called her this because she was His spouse, just as you are.

They asked her, "What is so special about your spouse?" They wondered about the urgency and passion of her request. People who are passionate about Christ are often misunderstood by those who serve Him from a distance. People will murmur against a sold-out worshiper. Intimate lovers of Christ are misunderstood, misjudged, and often mislabeled. For an example of a passionate worshipper who was misunderstood, read Mark 14:3–4. Below is my interpretation of verse 9:

KJV	MY VERSION
"What is thy beloved more than another beloved, O thou fairest among women? What is thy beloved more than another beloved, that thou dost so charge us?"	"Who is your Beloved that He is more special than another, O, you most beautiful among married women? Who is your Beloved that He is more special than another? Who is He that causes you to be in such distress?"

VERSE 10:

"My beloved is white and ruddy, the chiefest among ten thousand."

The bride begins to tell them who He is and why He is so special. She declares that He is *white,* which means "dazzling, glowing, clear, and bright." His purity and holiness are displayed by a literal brightness as in the transfiguration (Luke 9:28–32).

He is *ruddy*. This means his complexion contains red hues. Ruddy describes the characteristics of Nazarites (Henry). Jesus was a Nazarite, as was His ancestor David. 1 Samuel 16:12 shows that David's ruddy complexion was appealing.

She boldly declared He is "chiefest among ten thousand." *Chiefest* refers to the most significant banner of all banners. Jesus became a banner: "He is himself lifted up as a banner" (Isaiah 11:10). Jesus is the highest of all banners among ten thousand banners. *Ten thousand* is used in such a way as to communicate a great amount, uncountable, and even an infinite number. "He is higher than the kings of the earth" (Psalm 89:27).

Below is my interpretation of verse 10, where the bride describes her beloved to the daughters of Jerusalem:

KJV	MY VERSION
"My beloved is white and ruddy, the chiefest among ten thousand."	"My Beloved's purity is dazzling with brightness. His appearance is pleasing and appealing. His glory is of incomparable perfections and unparalleled worth. He is the most significant of all kings."

VERSE 11:

"His head is as the most fine gold, his locks are bushy and black as a raven."

Now she begins to describe specific things about Him. *Head* means a literal head, but it also refers to His leadership or His rule over her. "His head is as the most-fine gold" denotes pure gold; the best gold; shining gold, strong and solid gold. Like gold, Christ's glory is beautiful, valuable, and powerful. In Daniel 2:38, Nebuchadnezzar's monarchy was compared to a head of gold.

She tells them His *locks*, or hair (hair refers to glory), is bushy and black as a raven. *Bushy* means "mounded or heaped up and strong." Bushy comes from a root word meaning "exalted." Christ's glory is exalted, mounded and heaped up above every other glory. *Black* means "black," but comes from a root word meaning "the color of early dawn." His glory is as the dawn. It is still dark but full of the promise of color and beauty. *Raven* comes from a root word denoting the color of dusk as the sun sets. His glory is in the dusk as well. His glory does not change! James 1:17 tells us that there is no variation or shadow of turning with the Most High. "For I am the Lord, I change not" (Malachi 3:6). I've written verse 11 in more understandable words:

KJV	MY VERSION
"His head is as the most fine gold, his locks are bushy, and black as a raven."	"His rule over me is solid, strong, valuable and excellent. His glory does not change!"

VERSE 12:

"His eyes are as the eyes of doves by the rivers of waters, washed with milk, and fitly set."

Now she starts to describe His eyes, saying they are as "dove's" eyes. Doves have one mate for life. You might say they have eyes only for each other. The word *dove* comes from a root word that means "intoxicated by wine." So, gazing at Him intoxicates us and intoxicates Him as well. That makes me smile. We truly do not fathom the impact we have on Him.

These doves are by "rivers of waters." *Rivers* comes from a root word meaning "a current that gathers or pulls." His eyes are a current that captivates us and pulls us in. *Waters* comes from a root word that means "semen" (Strong). Readers, don't freak out! Simply put, this means His look or gaze captivates and impregnates us.

His eyes have been "washed with milk." *Milk* refers to the Word of God (1 Peter 2:2), and in this case it refers to the cream—the richest, fattest part of the milk (Strong). If His eyes are washed with milk, He sees me through His Word. He does not see me as I see myself or even as the world sees me. He sees me as valuable like cream. His eyes are "fitly set." This means to be settled as in a marriage covenant (Strong). It is to be content and not wandering. His eyes are fixed on us. We are His love. My rendition of verse 12:

KJV	MY VERSION
"His eyes are as the eyes of doves by the rivers of waters, washed with milk, and fitly set."	"His eyes are for me and me only; I am His mate for life. His eyes are like a current that pulls me into deep waters where I am impregnated by Him and thereby bear fruit for Him. His eyes see me through His Word, which makes me look valuable. They are focused on me and will not stray or wander."

VERSE 13:
"His cheeks are as a bed of spices, as sweet flowers: His lips like lilies, dropping sweet smelling myrrh."

Cheeks mean "soft." They indicate that His countenance emanates mercy as opposed to a set or clamped jaw, which would denote an angry countenance. *Bed* means "to be piled up." *Spices* refer to a fragrance. His mercy is piled up and smells like sweet flowers. His mercy romances us. It draws us into intimacy.

The Hebrew word for *lips* is "boundaries." Boundaries, especially spiritual boundaries, are established by our speech, by the words that our lips speak. Lilies are symbolic of life because they are plants that seem dead but spring back to life each year. Lips that are like lilies would speak life. Myrrh is a sweet-smelling fragrance symbolizing His grace for us. This phrase means His lips are speaking life and grace over us. A picture of grace being communicated is found when the father kissed his prodigal son. We need to be careful to speak life over ourselves, to agree with what He says about us in His Word. Here's my rendition of verse 13:

KJV	MY VERSION
"His cheeks are as a bed of spices, as sweet flowers: his lips like lilies, dropping sweet smelling myrrh."	"His mercy for me is piled up very high. Its fragrance is like sweet flowers. His mercy romances me. His lips are like beautiful lilies, which speak life over me while kissing me with the kiss of grace. My boundaries are grace and grace on every side."

VERSE 14:
"His hands are as gold rings set with the beryl: his belly is as bright ivory overlaid with sapphires."

This verse is a prime example of the necessity to keep a spiritual mind-set as you read and study Song of Solomon. The book and this verse contain hidden sexual connotations that must only be applied in the spirit realm to our intimate relationship with Jesus. So, hold on, this is about to get a little steamy.

His *hands* denote His power and strength. His power and strength are as "gold rings." This means they are valuable and solid; they shimmer and are glorious. His power and strength are glorious! Rings have often been associated with authority and power, like a king's ring. Christ's authority, power, and strength are valuable, solid, glorious, and absolute. "All power is given unto me in heaven and earth" (Matthew 28:18). Rings are round and turning. They are continuous, having no beginning or ending. Christ's authority and power has no beginning or end. He is omnipotent. He always has been and always will be. Rings also speak of the marriage covenant. His covenant with us is forever. A *beryl* is a gem or a precious stone. Christ is the precious cornerstone upon which our covenant with Him is established (Ephesians 2:19–20).

She even tells them about His *belly*. Recall the word *bowels* (verse 4), which means "the womb or uterus of a woman." *Belly* in this verse points to the male organ of reproduction (Strong). His reproductive organ is as "bright ivory," which refers to the sharp-pointed tusks of elephants. His reproductive organ is covered with *sapphires*. The Hebrew word for *sapphires* comes from a root word meaning, "to recount and retell as would a teacher or a scribe." Metaphorically, this is saying that His reproductive organ is His sharp-pointed teachings with which He penetrates our spirits again and again until we are impregnated to reproduce Himself. Wow! I'm undone! His teachings are conforming me into His image and causing me to bear fruit that looks like Him. Verse 14:

KJV	MY VERSION
"His hands are as gold rings set with the beryl: his belly is as bright ivory overlaid with sapphires."	"His power is glorious, limitless, valuable, and beautiful. His ability to reproduce in me and through me is marvelously achieved by beautiful and powerful teachings that are beyond value."

VERSE 15:

"His legs are as pillars of marble, set upon sockets of fine gold: his countenance is as Lebanon, excellent as the cedars."

She is still describing Him to the daughters of Jerusalem. *Legs* mean literal legs. They are like pillars or strong columns made of marble, which, according to *Strong's Concordance*, are white marble. These column-like legs sit on *sockets*, which translates to "foundation." The foundation is "of fine gold," which means pure gold, the best gold (shimmering, strong, and solid). Picture a man with massively strong legs, like a warrior or weight lifter. Now think about the fact that Christ, this strong man, is for you and not against you. It is both comforting and a little unnerving to get a glimpse of how powerful He is.

His countenance or appearance is as Lebanon, that white, snow-covered mountain range. The snow denotes purity, and *Lebanon* comes from a root word that means "to make white or pure". *Countenance* comes from a root word that means "heart." His heart is as "excellent as the cedars." The cedar tree is a very strong wood. It excels all other trees in height and strength (Henry). Trees are often used in the Bible to symbolize men (Mark 8:24; Isaiah 55:12). Jesus' heart is pure and excellent in every way when compared to other men. His appearance reveals His pure heart, which excels all other hearts in power and purity. And now, my presentation of verse 15:

KJV	MY VERSION
"His legs are as pillars of marble, set upon sockets of fine gold: his countenance is as Lebanon, excellent as the cedars."	"His legs are as massive columns of pure strength; His beautiful feet provide a strong and solid foundation. His appearance reflects His heart, which is pure and excellent in height and strength."

VERSE 16:

"His mouth is most sweet: yea, he is altogether lovely. This is my beloved, and this is my friend, O daughters of Jerusalem."

Mouth refers to the palate or tongue—the organ of taste, speech, and kissing. Yes, *Strong's Concordance* says kissing! The kiss of His mouth communicates grace, which is lovely. Where would we be without His kisses of grace? Recall everything that she has told them about Him and understand that He is "altogether lovely."

Beloved means "lover." He is her lover and her friend. *Friend* means a literal friend, husband, and lover; and it comes from a root word that means "one who rules over me as a friend." She knows Him so well that she boldly claims relationship to Him.

Here is my interpretation of verse 16, where she has been addressing rare daughters of peace:

KJV	MY VERSION
"His mouth is most sweet: yea, he is altogether lovely. This is my beloved, and this is my friend, O daughters of Jerusalem."	"The words of His mouth are sweet as milk to newborn babes, and sweet as honey to the mature. The kisses of His mouth are the sweetest tokens of grace and love. He is altogether delightful and desirable. This is my Beloved, and He is my friend, my husband, my lover. O daughters of Jerusalem. O rare daughters who rebuild peace."

While we leave chapter 5 with a beautiful and very powerful description of Jesus, sadly, we also leave it with the bride still separated from Him. Take heart, my friends, they will be reunited in chapter 6. For now, reread my presentation of verses 9–16, a brilliant description of Jesus, in words that should leave you in absolute awe of Him.

Reflections

What characteristic of Jesus stands out to you?

_____

_____

_____

_____

Verse 12 refers to Jesus' sperm, and verse 14 refers His organ of procreation. In your own words, explain what this means.

_____

_____

_____

_____

Response

Worship Jesus; adore Him based on the description given in this passage. Afterward, record your encounter with Him here.

_____

_____

_____

_____

_____

_____

_____

_____

WEEK SIX

Song of Solomon 5

AWAKEN TO HIS LOVE

During the time that I was searching out truth for this chapter, I had a vision. I saw my little white pillow. The pillow from my vision was in my bedroom, under the comforter, completely out of sight. But I saw the pillow. When the vision ended, I immediately began to seek the Lord regarding its message. I keep this little pillow on my bed with my regular pillow. I use it between my knees when I lay on my side or under my knees when I lay on my back, which takes the pressure off my lower back. This little white pillow is for pure comfort.

I believe that the vision of the small comfort pillow opens the meaning of Song of Solomon 5, where Jesus is knocking and calling for the church to *awaken* to His presence, but she is too comfortable. The church has been made comfortable by His abundant blessings in our lives. Verse 1 describes some of those blessings: "Eat, O friends; drink, yea, drink abundantly; O beloved."

Also, consider that many people are going through difficult circumstances, such as financial strain, troubled marriages, or serious problems with children, parents, or coworkers. Some have serious health problems. Could these things cause us to wake up to His presence?

He is present in every circumstance and every situation. He is there with you. The Word says He will never leave you or forsake you. Look for Him in your circumstance. Instead of looking to Him, we often use coping mechanisms. Ask Him where He is. He will reveal himself to you. He wants to be our comforter. He wants to be our rest. He wants us to cast our cares on Him. He will be our comfort if we only surrender to His love and peace.

I heard the Lord say: "Awaken to my love." We are often awake to duty, works, and religion but not to His love. Song of Solomon is about love. As individuals, we need to awaken to His love. We must stir ourselves out of slumber and out of our comfort zone. Put off our covering of religion and works. We need to open our hearts to His love. Open our hearts to His provision that makes us worthy of His love. Open our hearts to intimacy with Him. This needs to be our priority!

Now enjoy my rendition of Song of Solomon 5, with all the symbolism replaced and His words in italics.

> "*I have entered My garden; your spirit has become My garden.*
> *My beloved, you are part of Me.*
> *My bride, you are the one who completes Me*
> *and makes Me whole.*
> *I have gathered your prayers and your worship;*
> *they are a sweet fragrance to Me.*
> *O friends, O beloved, come eat with Me,*
> *I bring My Word to the table,*
> *It tastes like honeycomb;*
> *The honey becomes wisdom in your mouth.*
> *Drink, yes, drink deeply of all that I have for you.*
> *Drink milk, and when it no longer satisfies you,*

Drink of the wine of My spirit. Drink deeply.
Drink and be filled with joy. Drink and be healed.
Drink of all that I make available to you.
Drink deeply until you are intoxicated with My love.
I am indulging in sleep, my spirit is at ease and comfortable,
But suddenly my spirit wakes up. Whose voice is that?
It is the voice of my beloved.
My heart is exposed, my slumber and negligence obvious.
He is knocking on the door; He is calling for me.
Open your spirit, My beloved. You are part of Me.
Open your spirit, My love, My intimate friend.
Open your spirit, My dove, My only mate forever,
You make My heart glad and light.
Open your spirit, My undefiled, My perfect bride;
For I am overwhelmed with desire for you.
Consider the hardships I have endured to be intimate with you.
Consider the blood that covered my head and dripped from My hair.
Open your spirit, Let Me into your heart.
I cannot open to You because I have done my religious duties.
I have washed my feet; if I come to You, they will be soiled.
My lover powerfully touched my spirit with His grace.
My womb moaned for Him.
I was overwhelmed with the desire to be intimate with Him,
and reproduce for Him.
I rose to open my spirit to my lover.
I touched the lock and my hands dripped with grace to open the door.
My fingers were covered with His sweet-smelling fragrance.
I opened to my Beloved,
but my Beloved had withdrawn Himself and was gone.
Oh, why did I fail to respond when He called to me?
I sought Him with worship and prayer, but I could not find Him;

I had no sense of His favor, of His comfort, of His love.
I was thoroughly distraught.
I cried out to Him in worship and prayer,
I begged, but He did not answer me.
The evil principalities and powers
that are assigned to my destruction found me.
They attacked me, they hit me, they beat me, they tortured me.
They wounded, bruised and crushed my spirit.
Those evil principalities who watch for the vulnerable,
They violently exposed me and shamed me.
I charge you, rare daughters of peace, who rebuild and restore,
if you find my lover, tell Him that I am grieved, and sorry.
Tell Him His absence has left me weak and helpless.
Tell Him that I am lovesick for Him.
Who is your Beloved that He is more special than another?
O, you most beautiful among married women,
Who is your Beloved that He is more special than another?
Who is He that causes you to be in such distress?
My Beloved's purity is dazzling with brightness.
His appearance is pleasing and appealing.
His glory is of incomparable perfections
and unparalleled worth.
He is the most significant of all kings.
His rule over me is solid, strong, valuable and excellent.
His glory does not change!
His eyes are for me and me only;
I am His mate for life.
His eyes are like a current that pull me into deep waters
where I am impregnated by Him and thereby bear fruit for Him.
His eyes see me through His Word, which makes me look valuable.
They are focused on me and will not stray or wander.

He is firmly settled into His covenant with me.
His mercy for me is piled up very high,
Its fragrance is like sweet flowers. His mercy romances me.
His lips are like beautiful lilies,
which speak life over me while kissing me with the kiss of grace.
My boundaries are grace and grace on every side.
His power is glorious, limitless, valuable, and beautiful.
His ability to reproduce in me and through me is marvelously achieved
by beautiful and powerful teachings that are beyond value.
His legs are as massive columns of pure strength,
His beautiful feet provide a strong and solid foundation.
His appearance reflects His heart,
which is pure and excellent in height and strength.
The words of His mouth are sweet as milk to newborn babes
and sweet as honey to the mature.
The kisses of His mouth are the sweetest tokens of grace and love.
He is altogether delightful and desirable.
This is my Beloved, and He is my friend, my husband, my lover.
O daughters of Jerusalem. O rare daughters who rebuild peace."

Reflection and Response

If you are doing this as a group Bible study, use day five as the day you come together. Go over the refection questions from each day together. Share, encourage, and pray for one another.

_____

_____

If you are doing this study on your own, review the reflection and response sections from each day. Worship Him and ask Him to do an even deeper work. Ask Him to add another layer of truth and beauty to your heart. Afterward, record your experience with Him.

WEEK SEVEN

Song of Solomon 6:1–3

TRULY SATISFIED

A short review of chapter 5 will help us transition into this chapter. In Chapter 5:9, the daughters of Jerusalem asked the woman (the church, you) who her beloved is. Then the woman spends the next eight verses describing Him and who He is. She talks about His complexion, His head, His hair, His eyes, His cheeks, His hands, His belly, His legs, His countenance, and His mouth. It's all symbolic, very romantic, and very powerful. Chapter 5 ended with the bride summing up her description of Jesus to the daughters of Jerusalem, telling them that He is altogether lovely. Then chapter 6 opens with the daughters of Jerusalem asking the bride a question.

VERSE 1:
"Whither is thy beloved gone, O thou fairest among women? Whither is thy beloved turned aside? that we may seek him with thee."

These daughters are so impressed with her description of who He is that they ask, "Where is He? If He is that wonderful, then I want to know Him as you do." Our testimony of how much Jesus loves us can be so powerful that it makes others desire to know Him intimately. The verse says they want to seek Him. The lost need to find Him. Unless we tell them *who* He is and *where* He is, they cannot find Him. In my interpretation of verse 1, the daughters of Jerusalem are speaking:

KJV	MY VERSION
"Whither is thy beloved gone, O thou fairest among women? Whither is thy beloved turned aside? that we may seek him with thee."	"Where is your lover, Oh, most beautiful woman? Where has your lover gone? We only want to find Him, as you have."

VERSE 2:

"My beloved is gone down into his garden, to the beds of spices, to feed in the gardens, and to gather lilies."

The bride directs them to where He is, telling them He has gone into His garden. We learned earlier that the word *garden* indicates an enclosed and protected garden. It symbolizes your spirit, which is enclosed for your bridegroom and Him alone. It is a private place for the two of you. When we start to fellowship with Christ and know Him in our spirit, that's when we begin to understand the breadth, length, depth, and height of His love for us. Intimacy with Him takes place in our spirit. The garden enclosed, our spirit, is to be separated from the world. It is to be a place of intimate communion with Christ. He is in our spirit. It is a little Holy of Holies. He dwells in our spirit. We can learn to seek Him in our spirit. He is there. He is not far off. "I will never leave thee, nor forsake thee" (Hebrews 13:5). This verse holds the answer as to the whereabouts of the bridegroom in chapter 5. Recall that the woman did not quickly answer the knock; instead, she made excuses. Then she went looking for Him but could not find Him. Now, she realizes that He never left her. He was in her spirit. I believe He allowed her to feel as though He left her so that she would forsake religious works. When she described Him to the daughters of Jerusalem, her words became worship, which caused Him to manifest His presence to her. He was in her spirit or garden the whole time.

In the garden there is a "bed of spices." The *bed* symbolizes a place of sexual intimacy. Even though our intimacy with Jesus is in the realm of the spirit, the word *bed* is used to emphasize that intimacy is exactly what Jesus wants. The *spices* are a sweet smell released from the bed of our mutual love—the Savior's love for us and our love for Him. The phrase "to feed in the gardens" refers to a special friendship. *Feed* indicates a dear friend that meets and satisfies your needs. You will not only find Him in your spirit, but you will also find that He has prepared a table for you to feed at in your spirit (Psalm 23). This table is furnished with strength, joy, peace, righteousness, hope, and victory. People get depleted because they are not eating at His table. They eat at the enemy's table, which offers discouragement, despair, disappointment, and hopelessness. Christ will feed His special friends. He will also partake of what is in their spirit. Hopefully, your spirit offers Him spices. Spices are symbolic of thankfulness, praise, and worship. This feeding time is you partaking of Him and Him partaking of you. Notice that *gardens* in the phrase "to feed in the gardens" is plural. There are two spirits involved, yours and His. This feeding takes place in your spirit.

He is also gathering lilies in His garden. *Gather* means "gather," and *lilies* mean "to exult, rejoice, and display joy." Christ declared that He is the lily of the valley in Song of Solomon 2:1. When we studied that, we learned that lilies are white, which denotes Christ's purity. They are found in valleys or low places, which points to His humanity and humility.

(He came from heaven to earth.) Lilies also symbolize life because they seem to die in the winter but when spring comes, they live again. This is a picture of Christ's death for us and His resurrection. Since we were created in His image (Genesis 1:26) and are being conformed into His image (Romans 8:29), we can also be compared to a lily. We are pure because "He who knew no sin became sin; that we might become the righteousness of God" (2 Corinthians 5:21). Christ humbled Himself for our benefit. We are called to walk humbly, not think highly of ourselves, and to be servants (Mark 9:35, Philippians 2:3–7). When we walk humbly in His righteousness, knowing that we have none of our own, we are like the lilies of the valley. He gathers the lilies. He gathers us up. He gathers up His own. Notice the characteristics of these lilies: they exult, rejoice, and display joy. Does this describe you? It will if you feed on Him. Here is my rendering of verse 2 (the bride is speaking):

KJV	MY VERSION
"My beloved is gone down into his garden, to the beds of spices, to feed in the gardens, and to gather lilies."	"My lover is not gone away from me. He is in my spirit, a private enclosed place where we are intimate. He partakes of my love for Him and I partake of His love for me. We satisfy one another. He has made me beautiful and gathers me up as His own."

VERSE 3:
"I am my beloved's, and my beloved is mine:
he feedeth among the lilies."

Beloved means "lover." She declares that she belongs fully and completely to Him. Likewise, He belongs to her. I challenge you to say this out loud: "I belong fully and completely to Jesus. Jesus belongs fully and completely to me."

Let that truth sink in. Think about each word. He belongs totally, fully, and completely to you. She is saying, "We are lovers." Can you say that about yourself and Jesus? Try it. He feeds on you, on your spirit, on its fruit. The *eth* of *feedeth* makes it a verb that means "to feed and keep on feeding continuously." Remember that *feed* also refers to a special, dear friend that meets and satisfies your needs. He desires that your fellowship with Him is consistent, continual, and constant. Read on for my rendition of verse 3:

KJV	MY VERSION
"I am my beloved's, and my beloved is mine: he feedeth among the lilies."	"I am His and He is mine. Our fellowship is constant."

Go back through and reread my rendition of these verses. It is awesome when we realize that our intimacy with Jesus can be constant. Somehow, we satisfy Him, and He desires us deeply.

I want to bring some clarity regarding "the daughters of Jerusalem." The phrase means rare daughters who rebuild peace. However, in this chapter, they represent those who know Him in a shallow way, they have not pressed into intimacy with Jesus. They look at the relationship the Shulamite woman has with Him and they want that too.

Reflections

What happened that made the daughters of Jerusalem want to seek Jesus?

_____

_____

_____

Tell what each of the following symbolize:

Garden: _____

_____

_____

Bed of Spices: _____

_____

_____

Feeding: _____

_____

_____

Lilies: _____

_____

_____

Response

Spend some time with the only one who can satisfy you. Worship Jesus, partake of Him, and let Him partake of you. Afterward, record your experience with Him.

_____

_____

_____

_____

_____

_____

_____

_____

_____

_____

WEEK SEVEN

Song of Solomon 6:4–7

SPIRITUAL BEAUTY

Now Jesus is speaking to His beloved, to you and me. When we become more aware of our spirit and the fact that He is in our spirit for the purpose of continual and constant communion, we begin to hear His voice and His loving words for us.

VERSE 4:
"Thou art beautiful, O my love, as Tirzah, comely as Jerusalem, terrible as an army with banners."

He said, "Thou art beautiful." *Beautiful* means "beautiful." Then He calls you "His love," which means intimate friend. He says you are as beautiful as Tirzah, which is a city. The city's name means "delightful, favorable, pleasant, or acceptable."

He says you are as "comely as Jerusalem." *Comely* means "completely beautiful." Jerusalem is a beautiful place to live, but this is saying more than that. Jerusalem is called the joy of the whole earth. It is known as a holy city. Solomon's temple was there. The temple was a place of worship, a place of His presence, a place of extravagant beauty, and a place of holiness. Christ lives in us. We are His sanctuary. He makes us beautiful, completely beautiful. It's the beauty of holiness that radiates from us when His spirit enters our being. Your spirit is a beautiful place, a holy place, a place of worship, and a place of His presence. Just pause and think about that.

Furthermore, Psalm 122:3 refers to Jerusalem as "a city compact together," which means the city is complete, finished, sound, safe, uninjured, whole, good, restored, and in unity. This is how Christ sees you. He sees the completed work. He finished the work. When you are in unity with Him, you are complete, sound, safe, uninjured, whole, good, and restored. This blesses me. That's how He sees us, and that's how we are. We need to believe this truth.

Jerusalem is also associated with peace. Christ sees your spirit at peace. Because of Him, your spirit can be at peace. Colossians 3:15 says that we can choose to let the peace of Christ rule in our hearts. We can choose peace. If we neglect to be diligent in choosing peace, then fears, worries, and insecurities will creep in.

He says we are as "terrible as an army with banners." *Terrible* means "frightening and dreadful to look at." An army indicates the need for warfare. We must realize that we are called to do spiritual warfare. Ephesians 6:10–18 tells us about the necessity of warfare and presents the armor of God, including the sword of the spirit, which represents the spoken Word. We overcome by the blood of the Lamb and the word of our testimony (Revelation 12:11). The weapons of our warfare cast down imaginations (2 Corinthians 10:4-5). That's just a quick overview of spiritual warfare. Perhaps you need a more in-depth study of the topic. There are many good books on the subject, including *Putting on the Armor* by Pricilla Shirer.

Banners refer to a battle standard or flag that identifies the army. To the enemy, in the realm of the spirit, you look like an awesome warrior, absolutely frightening and dreadful. They see a battle standard that identifies you as belonging to Jesus Christ. They see faith! Faith terrifies our enemy. They see the armor of God, which is Christ in us, on us, and all around us. They hear the word of our testimony (our declarations) and know they are defeated. They cannot even attack us in our imaginations. Hallelujah! Here's my portrayal of Christ's words to us in verse 4:

KJV	MY VERSION
"Thou art beautiful, O my love, as Tirzah, comely as Jerusalem, terrible as an army with banners."	*"You are beautiful, My intimate friend. You are delightful, favorable, and pleasant. Your spirit is a holy, beautiful, peaceful place, which is completely whole and good. You are a mighty force in the spirit realm. You boldly carry My battle flag of victory and triumph."*

VERSE 5:
"Turn away thine eyes from me, for they have overcome me: Thy hair is as a flock of goats that appear from Gilead."

Verses 5–7 are almost word for word the same as Song of Solomon 4:1–5. He comments on her eyes, hair, teeth, and temples. He repeats what He said to her in chapter 4 because He wants her to know He still has the same opinions of her as He did before she yielded to religious works by refusing to let Him in the door (chapter 5). Now He is reassuring her that He still loves her and thinks the same about her. This is a picture of forgiveness, restoration, and justification (just as if I had never sinned). No wonder we love Him so much. "He who has been forgiven much, loveth much" (Luke 7:47). I don't know about you, but that describes me. I've been forgiven much and I love Him very much!

He instructs her not to look at Him but to turn her eyes away. Why? Because our look has *overcome* Him, or overwhelmed Him. He is overwhelmed by our love for Him. I don't think that He wants us to look away. I think that He is communicating the effect our loving gaze has on Him. It overwhelms Him.

He sees our hair as a "flock of goats." That's pretty weird, so let's review the symbolism regarding goats. They are clean animals. We are made clean by the blood of Jesus. Goats were useful for eating, milking, and sacrifice. Clothing and tents were made out of their hair and hide. We are useful to the Lord. A shepherd knows how many goats he has. Why? They represent wealth. So, if our hair is like a flock of goats, and according to Matthew 10:30 "the hairs of our heads are numbered," then He is speaking here about our value. He has made us clean. We are valuable and useful to Him.

These goats hung out on Mount Gilead, which was a rocky, craggy mountain. It was rough terrain, but goats are sure-footed on rough terrain. We, too, can be sure-footed in Christ, even on rough terrain or difficult situations (Habakkuk 3:19).

Proverbs 30:29–31 says, "Goats are comely going." *Comely* means "completely beautiful." Coming or going, they are beautiful. Deuteronomy 28 says that we "are blessed coming in or going out." What makes the goat beautiful to the shepherd? Value. Because of their value, they are a beautiful sight to the shepherd. And we, dear readers, are a valuable sight to our Shepherd, Jesus.

I want us to think about hair. For a woman, hair is symbolic of glory (1 Corinthians 11:15). Hair is also a head covering. When Christ looks at us, He sees His glory on us. He sees His glory covering us. He wants us to see and be aware of His glory on ourselves. His glory makes us beautiful, completely beautiful.

When I first began to study chapter 6, I had a dream. In the dream, my hair was soaking wet with thick blood. It was way beyond gross. I believe the interpretation of the dream is that He is my head covering. His blood is my glory. In Him I am completely beautiful. My rendition of Christ's words to us in verse 5:

KJV	MY VERSION
"Turn away thine eyes from me, for they have overcome me: Thy hair is as a flock of goats that appear from Gilead."	*"You are beautiful, Oh, My intimate friend, My delight. You are extravagantly beautiful; you are My joy. When you look at Me with such love, I am overwhelmed. I have numbered all your hairs because you are valuable to Me. Oh, My beloved, you are clean and desirable; and completely beautiful."*

VERSE 6:
"Thy teeth are like a flock of sheep that are even shorn, which came up from the washing; whereof everyone bears twins, and none is barren among them."

Again, this is identical to what He said about us in chapter 4. Let's do a quick review of the symbolism of these hilarious words. *Teeth* signify eating. Think about sheep and how they eat grass. They chew it again so that they can have proper digestion. Likewise, we eat the Word (Matthew 4:4). Just as the sheep ruminate the grass or cud, chewing it again, we are to meditate on the word of God or chew it again. We take in the Word and then meditate on it over and over again until the truth within that passage is absorbed into our spirit. That truth becomes more than just head knowledge. It is digested and affects who we are. This constant chewing on their cud makes the sheep's teeth even. Constantly meditating on the Word makes our spiritual teeth even, which indicates balanced theology or wisdom. Many teeth have names synonymous with wisdom: wisdom teeth, incisors (insight), eyeteeth (insight and understanding). Wisdom, which comes from meditating on the Word, makes us beautiful to the Lord. True intimacy with Jesus would never neglect reading, meditating on, and praying the Word because He is the Word (John 1:1,14).

These sheep "came up from the washing." In other words, they were washed in a river, stream, or lake. Meditating on the Word cleanses our heart and life. Ephesians 5:26 refers to the "washing of the water of the word." The Word cleans up our life.

"Every one of these sheep bears twins and none is barren among them" (Song of Solomon 6:6). The teeth or the mouth speaks; it witnesses and testifies. This brings forth fruit or disciples. Therefore, we are not spiritually barren. "Bears twins" speaks of a double portion. Our spoken words can bring us into a double portion, or greater fruitfulness. My interpretation of verse 6 looks like this:

KJV	MY VERSION
"Thy teeth are like a flock of sheep that are even shorn, which came up from the washing whereof everyone bears twins, and none is barren among them."	*"You've carefully balanced your life with wisdom; You have washed your soul with My Word, this has made you fruitful even to a double portion."*

VERSE 7:
"As a piece of pomegranate are thy temples within thy locks."

Here's a review of the symbolism in this verse. The pomegranate is a brownish-red fruit. When it is cut open red pods are revealed. "A piece" would come from a slice of pomegranate, thus revealing the red. *Temples* is derived from a Hebrew word that refers to the cheek area of the face. Christ is complimenting her red cheeks. This indicates a blushing or an innocence. It indicates humility and modesty.

Locks translate from Hebrew to English as "a veil, a head covering." Her blushing cheeks are hidden under her veil. This points to true humility and modesty. She even hides her humility instead of proclaiming it to the world. "Blessed are the poor in spirit, for theirs is the kingdom of God" (Matthew 5:3). Here is verse 7 presented in my words:

KJV	MY VERSION
"As a piece of pomegranate are thy temples within thy locks."	*"Yes, you are truly humble and beautifully modest. You please Me, beloved."*

He is attracted to you! He finds you beautiful! He stated many of these same truths in chapter 4, but He takes the time to say them again. He is restoring and healing all the damage done by the demonic spirits that assaulted her in chapter 5. As you go back and reread His words about yourself, let them restore and heal your heart of past hurts.

Reflections

What does restoration mean to you? What does it look like?

_____
_____
_____

Describe how you feel after reading Jesus' words about yourself?

_____
_____
_____

Response

Just worship Him. He adores you and wants to hear your voice. He wants to touch your heart. Try to hear Him speaking a specific word just to you. Afterward, describe your encounter with Him.

_____
_____
_____
_____

WEEK SEVEN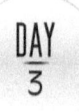

Song of Solomon 6:8–9

INCOMPARABLE BEAUTY

Jesus is still talking, telling His bride how beautiful she is. You are His bride; you are beautiful.

VERSE 8:
"There are threescore queens, and fourscore concubines, and virgins without number."

He begins to compare you to others. *Threescore* is sixty and *fourscore* is eighty. *Queens* refers to royalty, authority, beauty, and purpose (like Queen Esther). *Concubines* refer to the king's provision for his flesh. *Virgins* point to the innocent and desirable.

In this verse, He is listing beautiful, powerful, and desirable women. Beautiful women would include models and TV stars. Powerful women would include politicians, dignitaries, the wealthy, and those who are famous for their accomplishments. He is saying that even among all these, she is especially beautiful, powerful, desirable, and purposeful. He prefers her above all others. He continues with these declarations in verse 9, but first my presentation of verse 8:

KJV	MY VERSION
"There are threescore queens, and fourscore concubines, and virgins without number."	*"If all the beautiful women, even the most powerful women were gathered together."*

VERSE 9:

"My dove, my undefiled, is but one; She is the only one of her mother, she is the choice one of her that bare her. The daughters saw her, and blessed her; Yea, the queens and the concubines, they praised her."

Jesus is no longer addressing His beloved. He is addressing the daughters of Jerusalem. We know this because verse 9 reads, "She is the . . ." He is talking to those who look at her, admire her, and want what she has. He is communicating not only her beauty, but that they can also become His. They can become beautiful through Him.

My dove means "to effervesce" (sparkle, bubble up, overflow) like wine. *Wine* refers to the Holy Spirit. *Dove* also refers to Holy Spirit. This is a lovely picture of how when we are full of the Holy Spirit, we bubble up and overflow with the love and power of God.

Undefiled means "to be complete, to be finished, to be whole, to be entire, to be sound, to be unimpaired, to be upright, to be completely crossed over." We know all of this was accomplished by Christ in us. We need to realize that in Him we are complete, finished, whole, entire, sound, unimpaired, upright, and completely crossed over. We are a new creature in Him. Nothing missing, nothing broken.

The translation of "my dove, my undefiled, is but one" would read "is a holy one" (Henry). In Christ, we are holy. He is the one who sets us apart from all others.

The phrase: "She is the only one of her mother, she is the choice one of her that bare her" shows that she was specifically selected and chosen. "You have not chosen me, but I have chosen you" (John 15:16).

"The daughters saw her and blessed her; yea, the queens and the concubines, they praised her." This part of verse 9 shows that the chosen ones are esteemed by others. She excels them all. It is holiness that causes her to surpass them all in beauty and power and dignity. It is, of course, Christ in us that makes us beautiful, undefiled, complete, finished, and holy. It's important to acknowledge that we are holy. We are "holiness unto the Lord." The Old Testament priests would put on a *mitre* (turban or crown) that declared across their forehead: "Holiness unto the Lord" (Leviticus 8). In the New Testament, Revelation 14:1 shows us that in the realm of the spirit, believers have the Father's name on their foreheads. We are "holiness unto the Lord" not because of the Old Testament mitre, but because we are believers and followers of Jesus. When you realize that you are holiness unto the Lord, that's glory! That's beauty! That's power! Several years ago, when I first received the revelation that I am holiness unto the Lord, I started including that confession as I put on the armor of God. In Ephesians 6 we are told to put on the whole armor of God. When I put on the helmet of salvation and make appropriate declarations over my mind, I also declare that His name is on my forehead and that I am holiness unto the Lord. I can only make this declaration because of the blood of Jesus. His blood makes me beautiful! It makes me holy! It makes me powerful! All glory to His name! Following is my rendition of verses 8 and 9:

KJV	MY VERSION
"My dove, my undefiled, is but one; She is the only one of her mother, she is the choice one of her that bare her. The daughters saw her, and blessed her; Yea, the queens and the concubines, they praised her."	*"If all the beautiful women, even the most powerful women were gathered together, you, My only love, My precious pure bride, would still be the only one I want. You are the choicest! The other women bless you; they praise you. They want to be like you. They want what you have. They want Me."*

No one compares to Jesus. In this verse He is saying that no one compares to His bride. He prefers you above all others. Reread the translated verses with that in mind.

Reflections

2 Corinthians 10:12 says that we are not to compare ourselves with others. Christ compared us with others to show that we are the preferred. When we are tempted to compare ourselves with others, what is often the result? Why is that?

_____

_____

_____

_____

To what degree can you acknowledge that you are holiness unto the Lord?

___

Response

Praise Jesus for making you acceptable and even preferable. Thank Him for the beautification He has brought into your life. Ask Him to show you some things that you do not realize about yourself. Record what He shows you and what He says to you.

WEEK SEVEN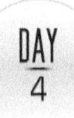

Song of Solomon 6:10–13
YOU'RE A TERRIBLE ARMY

*I*n these verses, Jesus is exclaiming her beauty and its effect on Him. There is a lot of symbolism locked up in these verses. Let's get the key, His Word, and unlock it so that we can understand what He is saying to us.

VERSE 10:
"Who is she that looketh forth as the morning, fair as the moon, clear as the sun, and terrible as an army with banners?"

Morning is when the sun rises. It appears as a great light. The church in the world is to be a light that dispels darkness. We, as individuals, are to be lights in the world, dispelling darkness. She "looketh forth" as the morning. This means to have heaven's perspective. To realize that it's a new day with new mercies and a new beginning. We are not only to be lights to the world but also, we are to see things from heavens perspective—to see the new mercies of God every day and to see the new beginnings God has for us. That's pretty awesome. To dive deeper into this truth, check out Matthew 13:43.

"Fair as the moon" is another aspect of our beauty. The moon rules over the night with a bright white light that is a reflection of the sun. Our light is a reflection of Christ. The sun rules over the day and the moon rules over the night (Psalm 136:8–9). We are to rule, to walk in spiritual authority and dominion in this dark world. We are called to spiritual warfare, to be militant.

Focus on the word *clear* in the phrase "clear as the sun." *Clear* means "pure, purified, or clean." Think about how the sun is a ball of fire and how we are purified by fire (1 Peter 4:12; Malachi 3:2).

Jesus said we are as "terrible as an army with banners." I'm sure you remember from verse 4 that *terrible* means "frightening, dreadful to look at." *Banners* refer to a battle standard, like a flag that identifies the army. Christians must never forget that they are called to spiritual warfare. In the realm of the spirit, you look like an awesome warrior, absolutely frightening and dreadful. We have a battle standard that identifies us as belonging to the Most High. Here is my rendition of verse 10:

KJV	MY VERSION
"Who is she that looketh forth as the morning, fair as the moon, clear as the sun, and terrible as an army with banners?"	*"You appear like a glorious sunrise which demonstrates My new mercies each and every day. You reflect My glory even as the moon reflects that of the sun. Alongside Me, you rule over the darkness. Yes, you are a mighty military force against the enemy."*

VERSE 11:

"I went down into the garden of nuts to see the fruits of the valley, and to see whether the vine flourished, and the pomegranates budded."

Oftentimes, in a warfare situation as well as in times of refining trials, it seems as if He has removed Himself. We are fighting for a breakthrough! Where is Jesus? Remember the words: "I will never leave you, nor forsake you" (Hebrews 13:5). However, it seems He hides His presence from us. We may ask, "Where are You?" In this verse, Jesus seems to be explaining where He was.

The garden is symbolic of your spirit. Christ visits your spirit. Nuts are a product of the garden or a fruit of your spirit that Christ wants to see. The valley indicates a low place. What fruit is your spirit producing in the emotionally or physically low place? Jesus is checking whether the vine flourishes. Is there life, spiritual life? Are the pomegranates budding? Pomegranates symbolize our humility and His holiness. Do you produce praise in hard times? "Though He slay me, yet will I praise Him" (Job 13:15).

My portrayal of verse 11:

KJV	MY VERSION
"I went down into the garden of nuts to see the fruits of the valley, and to see whether the vine flourished, and the pomegranates budded."	*"I have been in your spirit even when it was surrounded by anguish and trouble. And I saw there the beauty of holiness; I saw life and life abundant. You are a victorious woman!"*

VERSE 12:

"Or ever I was aware, my soul made me like the chariots of Amminadib."

Henry writes about the phrase "Or ever I was aware." Jesus is so overwhelmed by the fruit of her spirit "that yet He could not long content Himself with this, but suddenly felt a powerful, an irresistible, inclination in His bosom to manifest His presence to her."

Chariots offered a swift mode of transportation. Acknowledging His desire for her, He quickly manifests His presence to her. He was as swift as a chariot in getting to her. *Amminadid* means "my willing people who ride swiftly." Our willingness, faith, hope, desires, prayers, and expectations become a metaphorical chariot on which He can come to us quickly. That's what I want—for Him to come to me quickly. My exposition of verse 12:

KJV	MY VERSION
"Or ever I was aware, my soul made me like the chariots of Amminadib."	*"Oh, I am truly overwhelmed with the fruit of your spirit. I desire to manifest My presence to you now. I cannot get to you fast enough."*

VERSE 13:
"Return, return, O Shulamite; Return, return, that we may look upon thee. What will ye see in the Shulamite? As it were the company of two armies."

He comes back to her swiftly and now calls for her return, for her to come into His presence. She is invited, implored, even urged to "return," as the word is repeated three more times. *Shulamite* means "a perfectly peaceful one" and refers to the bride, to the church, to you and me. She is invited to return and recover the peace that has been lost and forfeited by her trial and His perceived absence. He wants to "look upon her" or to "see her face." He wants her to go no longer with her face covered like a mourner or like a person who has been shamed (Job 22:26; Hebrews 4:16).

The bridegroom, our Jesus, asks: "What will ye see in the Shulamite?" This phrase evokes two trains of thought from Bible scholars. First is the thought of unworthiness, lack of comeliness, or perhaps shame due to the bloodiness of two armies engaged in battle with her in the middle of the slaughter. This is supported by Song of Solomon 5:7, where the watchmen had smitten and wounded her. She now carries the marks of those wounds on her face, causing her to hide it. In chapter 1:6 she asked not to be looked at because she was black (with sin). Here she hides her face because she is bloody. This may denote the constant struggle that is between grace and corruption in the souls of believers. Grace and corruption, as two armies, continually skirmish within her, making her ashamed to show her face.

The second train of thought (and the one I agree with) is that this refers to her bridegroom, our Jesus, giving an account of her: "I will tell you what you shall see in the Shulamite; you shall see as noble a sight as that of two armies, not only as an army with banners but as two armies" (Henry).

Jesus says we are like "the company of two armies." The Hebrew meaning of *company* is a "dance company." It comes from a root word that means "a plan or strategy." Dance is a strategy and a weapon of spiritual warfare. So, we see the dance of two armies. Read below for my rendering of verse 13:

KJV	MY VERSION
"Return, return, O Shulamite; Return, return, that we may look upon thee. What will ye see in the Shulamite? As it were the company of two armies."	*"I am here; Come to Me, Beloved, Come and enjoy My presence. Let others see you, My beloved. What will they see? A victorious woman, as victorious as two mighty armies."*

Because of His blood, His resurrection, and His victory, we are invincible. He overcame sin and death for us; therefore "we are more than conquerors through Him that loved us" (Romans 8:37).

This is what we look like in the realm of the spirit. We radiate Jesus to the world. Each one of us looks like two armies to the enemy. Why do we look like two armies? Perhaps it's because we are not alone. Christ is standing right beside us. Wow! Go back and reread the translated verses about how you look in the realm of the spirit.

Reflections

In your own words, how does Jesus see you?

_____

_____

_____

Read Psalm 149. What type of warfare is the chapter talking about? What does Psalm 149:3 have in common with the meaning of *company* from Song of Solomon 6:13?

_____

_____

_____

Response

Worship the One who makes your victory and breakthrough possible, the One comes to you swiftly. Record your encounter with Jesus here.

_____

_____

_____

_____

_____

_____

_____

_____

_____

_____

_____

_____

_____

WEEK SEVEN

Song of Solomon 6

SPIRITUAL WARFARE

I believe that this particular chapter of Song of Solomon is about spiritual warfare. He impresses upon her the importance, necessity, and effectiveness of spiritual warfare because of her encounter with the demonic watchmen in chapter 5:7. The watchmen found her, wounded her, and took away her veil. This was an act of violence against her. It left her bloody, wounded, shamed, and fearful.

He begins the chapter by examining her spirit. Remember how the daughters of Jerusalem said, "Where is He?" We read how He was in the garden, or her spirit. He was examining her spirit to see the damage caused by the watchmen. Then He speaks healing and restoration to her spirit by reminding her who she is. I want us to look at verse 4 again.

VERSE 4:
"You are beautiful, my intimate friend. You are favorable, pleasant, and acceptable. Your spirit is a holy, beautiful, peaceful place, which is completely whole and good. You are a mighty force in the spirit realm. You boldly carry my battle flag of victory and triumph."

He continues to speak words of healing and restoration to her eyes, her hair, her teeth, and her cheeks. He speaks words that heal and restore her to who she was and what she believed back in chapter 4. He goes beyond the words in chapter 4 by comparing her to an army in chapter 6.

In verse 4 He refers to a battle flag that she carries into victory. In verse 10 she is like the sun that rules over the day, denoting authority. Still, in verse 10 she is terrible as an army with banners. Then we read in verse 13: "What will we see?" Someone who has been beaten and is bloody? No, He has restored her. She is now rejoicing and dancing. Her warfare is as powerful as two armies!

There is a powerful personal application in this chapter. Maybe you have just come through an attack. Perhaps due to your foolishness, you became vulnerable to the enemy. Or, perhaps, he just attacked you. Christ wants to restore all that you were before the attack. He wants to impart, a greater measure to you than you had before. Let Him speak the words of this chapter over you. As you read this rendition of Song of Solomon chapter 6, where the symbolism has been dissected and the metaphors have been discovered, thus laying bare the meaning and reality of His work in our lives, let Him restore and heal your spirit (His words are in italics):

"Where is your lover, oh most beautiful woman?
Where has your lover gone? We only want to find him, as you have.
My lover is not gone away from me.
He is in my spirit, a private enclosed place where we are intimate.
He partakes of my love for Him, and I partake of His love for me.
We satisfy one another.
He has made me beautiful and gathers me up as His own.
I am His and He is mine. Our fellowship is constant.
You are beautiful, My intimate friend.
You are delightful, favorable, and pleasant.

Your spirit is a holy, beautiful, peaceful place,
which is completely whole and good.
You are a mighty force in the spirit realm.
You boldly carry my battle flag of victory and triumph.
You are beautiful, Oh My intimate friend, My delight.
You are extravagantly beautiful; you are My joy.
When you look at Me with such love, I am overwhelmed.
I have numbered all your hairs because you are valuable to Me.
Oh, My beloved, you are clean and desirable; and very beautiful.
You've carefully balanced your life with wisdom;
You have washed your soul with My Word,
this has made you fruitful even to a double portion.
Yet, you are truly humble and beautifully modest.
You please Me, beloved.
If all the beautiful women, even the most powerful women,
were gathered together,
You, My only love, My precious pure bride,
would still be the only one I want.
You are the choicest!
The other women bless you; they praise you.
They want to be like you.
They want what you have. They want Me.
You appear like a glorious sunrise,
which demonstrates My new mercies each and every day.
You reflect My glory, even as the moon reflects that of the sun.
Alongside Me, you rule over the darkness.
Yes, you are a mighty military force against the enemy.
I have been in your spirit
even when it was surrounded by anguish and trouble.
And I saw there the beauty of holiness;
I saw life and life abundant.

You are a victorious woman!
Oh, I am truly overwhelmed with the fruit of your spirit.
I desire to manifest My presence to you now!
I cannot get to you fast enough.
I am here; Come to Me Beloved,
Come and enjoy My presence.
Let others see you, My beloved.
What will they see?
A victorious woman,
as victorious as
two mighty armies."

Reflection and Response

If you are doing this as a group Bible study, use day five as the day you come together. Go over the refection questions from each day together. Share, encourage, and pray for one another.

_____
_____
_____
_____
_____
_____

If you are doing this study on your own, review the reflection and response sections from each day. Worship Him and ask Him to do an even deeper work. Ask Him to add another layer of truth and beauty to your heart. Afterward, record your experience with Him here.

WEEK EIGHT

Song of Solomon 7:1–3

SPIRITUAL BEAUTY

This chapter begins with the bridegroom describing his bride. Christ talks about the church and you as an individual. He uses very intimate and personal words like thigh, navel, belly, and breasts. Certain phrases are hilarious, such as: "Thy belly is like a heap of wheat set about with lilies." Once we unlock the meaning, I believe that you will be extremely blessed by this passage.

<u>**VERSE 1:**</u>
"How beautiful are thy feet with shoes, O prince's daughter! The joints of thy thighs are like jewels, The work of the hands of a cunning workman."

The intimate and personal words used within this text are even more personal in the original Hebrew. I want to assure you now (before you read them) that I did the research, and what I present is theologically sound and true.

The word *beautiful* looks like an adjective, but it is a verb that means "to make oneself beautiful, to beautify." *Feet* refers to the tapping sound a footstep makes when one is wearing shoes. *Shoes* just means shoes. The word *prince* refers to a noble one. *Daughter* refers to a daughter by birth or adoption; it denotes a woman as well as a description of appropriate character for a daughter. Psalm 45:13 says, "The king's daughter is all glorious within." The verse indicates that Jesus finds our walk beautiful because we have allowed our character to be influenced by (and to reflect) our noble Father in heaven.

The next sentence is where it gets very personal with talk about our "joints" and "thighs." The meaning of these two words in the original Hebrew made my jaw drop. While our joints allow for smooth movement, the word means curves. Thighs are strong muscles and can mean one of two things. It can mean the outside of the leg where the sword was hung; or it can refer to the inside of the leg, the loin, where the seat of procreative power resides. Due to the subject of creation being established within the verse, I believe the intended meaning of *thighs* in this passage is "the seat of procreation." The meaning of *jewels* is "ornament." Referring to the God of all creation, the bridegroom then declares that she is the work or creation of a master workman, an artisan. Verse 1 would translate as follows:

KJV	MY VERSION
"How beautiful are thy feet with shoes, O prince's daughter! The joints of thy thighs are like jewels, The work of the hands of a cunning workman."	*"The sound of your footsteps, the way you carry yourself is beautiful, you have become a true daughter, your walk reflects the character of your Father. Like your Father, you possess the graceful, ornamental power to create life. You are indeed beautiful, the creation of God, Most High."*

VERSE 2:

"The navel is like a round goblet, which wanted not liquor: Thy belly is like an heap of wheat set about with lilies."

This is what my research discovered: *Navel* means "navel or umbilical cord." *Round* means "round." *Goblet* means "a bowl, or the curves and dips of the human body." *Liquor* comes from a root word, meaning "water mixed with wine." *Belly* means "abdomen or womb." *Heap* is a pile. *Wheat* is a food staple. *Lilies* (those beautiful flowers) derive from a root word that means "to exult in joy."

I couldn't quite fathom what this verse is saying. After seeking the Lord in prayer, the following thoughts came to me. This is about the woman's innermost cravings or desires. She does not want water mixed with wine as referred to in Isaiah 1:22. We learned in Song of Solomon 1:2 that Christ's love is better than wine. To mix water with it would be to dilute His love with other passions. This bride is praised because she does not want to dilute or mix the wine with anything else. His love satisfies her innermost being.

Her belly is full of wheat, which is a staple of good health. The wheat is surrounded by lilies, or beauty and joy. I believe this means she has filled her innermost being with His love, resulting in spiritual health, beauty, and joy. My translation of verse 2:

KJV	MY VERSION
"The navel is like a round goblet, which wanted not liquor: Thy belly is like an heap of wheat set about with lilies."	*You deeply desire My love and My love alone. My love nourishes you, making you spiritually healthy, beautiful and full of joy."*

VERSE 3:

"Thy two breasts are like two young rows that are twins."

This verse is identical in wording and meaning to Song of Solomon 4:5. The word *breasts* literally refers to a woman's breasts. They are often associated with comfort, compassion, and beauty. Breasts feed and nurture our children. Spiritually, we are nurses to the children of God: feeding, teaching, and equipping them to live victoriously. Our breasts are compared to a young roe. A *roe* is a female deer, goat, or gazelle. The meaning of twins not only refers to the obvious fact that women have two breasts, but it also speaks of balance, meaning our theology, what we teach and feed others, is balanced. It is not lopsided or out in left field. Here is my interpretation of verse 3:

KJV	MY VERSION
"Thy two breasts are like two young rows that are twins."	*"You are beautifully balanced; Able to comfort, teach, and nourish others with My love."*

We unlocked the meaning of all those intimate words! Go back and reread my rendition of this passage in words that you can understand. Jesus is speaking to you.

Reflections

Who is the cunning workman referred to in verse 1?

_____

_____

_____

_____

God is the Creator. You are made in His image. What does this mean in the physical realm? What does this mean in the spiritual realm?

_____

_____

_____

_____

Do you mix anything with His love? Do you crave other things to satisfy your soul?

_____

_____

_____

_____

Response

Pour your heart out to Him in worship and prayer. Let Him satisfy you and fill you with Himself. Afterward, record your experience with Him here.

_____

_____

_____

_____

_____

_____

_____

_____

_____

_____

_____

_____

_____

WEEK EIGHT

Song of Solomon 7:4–6

DECKED OUT!

Christ is still speaking of His adoration for you and for His church. In verses 1–3, He covered you from your breasts to your feet. Now He addresses your neck, your head, and your hair.

VERSE 4:
"Thy neck is a tower of ivory, eyes like the fish-pools in Heshbon, by the gate of Bathrabbim: thy nose is as the tower of Lebanon which looketh toward Damascus."

The first phrase is almost identical to Song of Solomon 4:4. The Hebrew word for *neck* refers to "binding the neck." The neck is compared to a "tower." *Ivory* means "sharp and pointed." You might remember seeing pictures of ancient Egyptian women with their necks wrapped in binding to elongate them, causing them to look something like a tower. The look was perceived as elegant, beautiful, and also indicated royalty.

Eyes in this verse means "eyes." The word *fish-pools* means "a reservoir" and comes from a root word meaning "to kneel and adore."

Heshbon is a place, but the meaning of the word points to "intelligence or the ability to reason." *Strong's Concordance* divides *Bathrabbim* into two words: *bath*, meaning "daughter" and *rabbim*, meaning "of abundance." The fact that she fixes her gaze on Him, that she kneels before Him in adoration, indicates her intelligence and brings her into a place of abundance.

The next phrase in this verse refers to the *nose*, and it means "passionate breathing." As we discovered in chapter 5, *Lebanon* refers to a snow-covered mountain, symbolizing our salvation experience where our scarlet sins became as white as snow.

Damascus is known as the place of Saul's conversion (Acts 9:1–25) and as the center of Christianity before it spread to other regions (Acts 9:20). Perhaps the phrase "thy nose is as the tower of Lebanon which looketh toward Damascus" means the woman is still passionate and excited about her salvation experience, which established her as His. Putting all of this together, I came up with the following interpretation of verse 4.

KJV	MY VERSION
"Thy neck is a tower of ivory, eyes like the fish-pools in Heshbon, by the gate of Bathrabbim: thy nose is as the tower of Lebanon which looketh toward Damascus."	*"I love the way you position your neck to fix your gaze on Me. Your eyes are like deep reservoirs of adoration for Me; They reflect great wisdom which has brought you to a place of abundance as a daughter of the King. You still passionately cherish your salvation experience, the day you became Mine."*

VERSE 5:

"Thine head upon thee is like Carmel, And the hair of thine head like purple; the king is held in the galleries."

Head and hair are the focus of this verse. *Head* refers to the "chief" or the "one in charge." In this case it's the mind. *Carmel* denotes a purposely planted and well-kept, fruitful garden or vineyard. Think about how necessary it is to thoughtfully and purposely program your mind with truth and to monitor its thoughts. The Hebrew word for *hair* in this verse means hair that has been "let down." Keep in mind that in Hebraic times, a woman only let down her hair in times of intimacy with her lover. Purple is associated with a royal lineage. Hair also refers to a woman's glory (1Corinthians 11:15). *King* refers to King Solomon or (in the case of this allegory) to Jesus, the King of kings. The word *galleries* is translated as "ringlets of hair." Put all of this together for an interpretation of verse 5:

KJV	MY VERSION
"Thine head upon thee is like Carmel, And the hair of thine head like purple; the king is held in the galleries."	*"Your mind is very pleasing to Me: You've purposely programmed it with truth and are vigilant to guard its thoughts. You have allowed yourself to be intimate with Me; This has created such glory all around you. Even though I'm the King, I'm captivated by you."*

VERSE 6:

"How fair and how pleasant art thou, O love, for delights!"

The King goes on to tell her why He is captivated by her. *Fair* means "beautiful, bright, with layers of beauty." *Pleasant* refers to character or behavior and means she behaves pleasantly or sweetly. He calls her *love*, the object of His affection. The word *delights* expresses exquisite pleasure. My translation of verse 6:

KJV	**MY VERSION**
"How fair and how pleasant art thou, O love, for delights!"	*"You are decked in layers of beauty; You are so sweet and pleasant to be around, Oh, My love, I take exquisite pleasure in you!"*

As you reread verses 4–6, realize that this is how Jesus sees and feels about you.

Reflections

In this passage, what position of the neck pleases Jesus?

_____

_____

_____

In this passage, where are the eyes focused?

_____

_____

In your own words, what does verse 5 mean?

___

___

___

Response

Position yourself as described in the passage. Worship Him, adore Him, be intimate with Him, experience His glory, and captivate Him with your love. Afterward, record your experience with Him here.

___

___

___

___

___

___

___

WEEK EIGHT

Song of Solomon 7:7–9

A SAMPLING

Jesus is still speaking. The phrases are very intimate. He takes hold of her breasts. He states that her mouth tastes like wine, which indicates a very passionate kiss. Keep in mind that Christ's love for us is not sexual. We are going to find out what this means and apply it in the realm of the spirit.

VERSE 7:
"This thy stature is like to a palm tree,
And thy breasts to clusters of grapes."

This verse required more prayer from me than study. Every keyword, except for palm tree, means exactly what it says. *Palm tree* comes from a root word that means "erect." The bridegroom or the King is admiring her upright character or her virtue. He is commenting on her fruit. Palm trees bear fruit that looks like berries or grapes. Galatians 5 lists the fruit of the Spirit that we as Christians should be demonstrating by our walk. *Breasts* means literal "breasts" and refers to the nurturing of others. My take on this verse is that her erect (upright) walk bears fruit as does her nurturing of others.

KJV	MY VERSION
"This thy stature is like to a palm tree, And thy breasts to clusters of grapes."	*"Your upright, virtuous character bears much fruit; Your compassionate nurturing of others displays an abundance of desirable fruit."*

VERSE 8:
"I said, I will go up to the palm tree, I will take hold of the boughs thereof: Now also thy breasts shall be as clusters of the vine, And the smell of thy nose like apples."

The verse describes shaking the branches of a palm tree so that fruit falls off and can be eaten. He is inspecting and sampling her fruit, the fruit of her spirit. *Boughs* refer to the extensions of a tree. For us, that would indicate the work of our hands and our walk. He samples the fruit we produce in our work and in our walk. The breasts refer to our compassionate nurturing of the young. He tastes that fruit too. He finds the fruit of our spirit abundant and pleasing. The *nose* in this verse refers to the place breath enters and exits the body, thereby sustaining life. The smell of life as opposed to death is a sweet, pleasant smell. The smell of death is most unpleasant. He finds only life in her. My interpretation of verse 8 is as follows:

KJV	MY VERSION
"I said, I will go up to the palm tree, I will take hold of the boughs thereof: Now also thy breasts shall be as clusters of the vine, And the smell of thy nose like apples."	*"I must sample this most desirable fruit, the fruit of your works and walk, the fruit of your compassionate nurturing. I find your fruit abundant and most satisfying. While sampling your fruit, I noticed the sweet fragrance of life all around you."*

VERSE 9:

"And the roof of thy mouth like the best wine for my beloved, that goeth down sweetly, causing the lips of those that are asleep to speak."

The phrase "the roof of thy mouth" refers to the words she speaks. The word *best* means "beneficial to one's welfare." *Wine* comes from a root word that means "to effervesce, make vivacious and enthusiastic." Wine makes the heart light and glad. Our words should do that. Wine has a reviving and refreshing effect. The words we speak should be like wine for our own benefit. The reason I say your words should benefit you is because He says they are beneficial "for my beloved." That's you and me. We are His beloved. *Sweetly* means "equity (fairness, justness, upright) and smoothness." Our words should be both upright in every way and easy to receive or smooth, like a smooth talker. Such words will cause those that are asleep or spiritually unenlightened to become enlightened. They, too, will then begin to speak appropriately.

KJV	MY VERSION
"And the roof of thy mouth like the best wine for my beloved, that goeth down sweetly, causing the lips of those that are asleep to speak."	*"The words you speak please Me. They are beneficial for your welfare, your prosperity, and your happiness. They are just, fair, pleasant and easy to receive. Your words cause others to speak appropriately."*

The truths that are hidden in Song of Solomon often blow me away. Reread and enjoy my translation of verses 7–9. All the symbolism has been replaced with words that we can apply to our relationship with Jesus. Remember that He is speaking these words to you.

Reflections

Which parts of the symbolism in this passage amazes you?

_____
_____
_____

How important are the words you say? Why?

_____
_____
_____

Response

Worship Him and let Him sample your fruit. Record what He says to you.

WEEK EIGHT

Song of Solomon 7:10–13
OPEN AND WILLING

Up until verse 10, the bridegroom has been speaking, telling His bride how she pleases Him. Now the bride begins to speak.

VERSE 10:
"I am my beloved's, and his desire is toward me."

She declares that she belongs to Him, calling Him her Beloved. After hearing all His praises of her, she is convinced that He desires her. We need to be convinced that He desires us and sees us as described in verses 1–9. We need to let these truths sink in so we can declare that He desires to be intimate with us as individuals. If we are lacking in any element of spiritual beauty, then let us more diligently and earnestly pursue it. Even as a woman fixes her hair or applies makeup to enhance her physical beauty, so must we attend to:

the uprightness of our walk (verses 1–8)
making sure it is His love alone that we desire (verse 2)
our theology, making sure that it is balanced (verse 3)
keeping our eyes on Him (verse 4)
reprograming our minds (verse 5)
the fruit of our spirit (verses 7–8)
the words which we speak (verses 8–9)

These specific factors and our attention to them add layers of beauty to our spirit, which make us desirable to Him. My rendition of verse 10 follows:

KJV	MY VERSION
"I am my beloved's, and his desire is toward me."	"I am my Beloved's, And He has convinced me that He desires me. I am desirable."

VERSE 11:
"Come, my beloved, let us go forth into the field; let us lodge in the villages."

She desires intimacy with Him and thus invites Him on a walk into the fields where they can be alone and intimate. This is a spiritual intimacy that is achieved through prayer, worship, and just enjoying His presence. She wants them to stay overnight in the villages where they always have quick access to the field and where they can be uninhibited in their intimacy.

KJV	MY VERSION
"Come, my beloved, let us go forth into the field; let us lodge in the villages."	"Come, my beloved Bridegroom, let us go where we can be alone and intimate with one another. And when we must return to public places, let us choose a place that affords us easy access to alone time where we may be intimate."

VERSE 12:

"Let us get up early to the vineyards; let us see if the vine flourish, whether the tender grapes appear, and the pomegranates bud forth: there will I give thee my loves."

She invites Him into her vineyard, which represents her spirit. She purposely exposes her spirit to Him, thereby pollinating herself with His virtues (Henry) so that she can produce the fruit of the spirit (Galatians 5:22). This is a time of loving on one another. She worships and adores Him. He, in turn, pollinates her fruit. She prefers to do this early so that they can have the vineyard to themselves. Several places in Scripture indicate an early morning seeking is best. "Those that seek me early shall find me" (Proverbs 8:17). My translation of verse 12 is as follows:

KJV	MY VERSION
"Let us get up early to the vineyards; let us see if the vine flourish, whether the tender grapes appear, and the pomegranates bud forth: there will I give thee my loves."	"Come with me to inspect the fruit of my soul and spirit. In the deepest part of my soul, I long to know You. In the hidden places of my spirit I will love and worship You."

VERSE 13:

"The mandrakes give a smell, and at our gates are all manner of pleasant fruits, new and old, which I have laid up for thee, O my beloved."

Keep thinking of fruit as it refers to the fruit of the spirit described in Galatians 5:22. *Mandrakes*, according to *Strong's Concordance*, are a "love-apple said to excite sexual desire and increase the likelihood of procreation." *Smell* is "a delightful fragrance or scent much like an alluring perfume." The fruit we produce should draw Christ to our spirits. We must desire to produce new fruit or new levels of fruit (new levels of love, joy, peace). The old level of fruit is good, but we must constantly reach for more excellent fruit. *Laid up* means "hidden" like a treasure in a secret place. This speaks of not putting our fruit on display for all to see. We should do good works (produce good fruit) even when no one can see. It is laid up for Him alone. Verse 13, in my words:

KJV	MY VERSION
"The mandrakes give a smell, and at our gates are all manner of pleasant fruits, new and old, which I have laid up for thee, O, my beloved."	"Notice the fragrance of our love, Notice the fruit our love produces. It enhances every area of our relationship, and is most pleasant. New fruit heaped upon the old. I have hidden fruit for only You to behold and partake of, my Beloved."

Wow, this bride is wide open to her bridegroom's love. That's how I want to be with Jesus. It may seem scary and vulnerable to you, but I assure you that you can trust Jesus. Please go back and reread my rendition of this passage. The bride is talking, so make it personal by saying the words to Jesus.

Reflections

How does the revelation that Jesus desires intimacy with you make you feel?

_____
_____
_____
_____

To what degree are you willing to completely open up and allow Him to inspect the fruit of your spirit?

Response

Do it. Worship Him. Invite Him into your spirit. Walk with Him through your spirit. Give Him your love. Let Him discover hidden fruit and love on you. Record your experience with Jesus here. Record what He shows you and what He says to you.

WEEK EIGHT

Song of Solomon 7

DESIRE

Song of Solomon 7 begins with the bridegroom (Christ) observing and declaring the spiritual beauty of His bride (the church, you, myself). Eventually the bride begins to believe His endearing words and develops a strong desire to be intimate with Him. Enjoy my rendition of chapter 7:

"The sound of your footsteps,
The way you carry yourself is beautiful,
You have become a true daughter;
Your walk reflects the character of your Father.
Like your Father, you possess the graceful,
ornamental power to create life.
You are indeed beautiful, the creation of God, Most High.
You deeply desire My love and My love alone.
My love nourishes you, making you spiritually healthy,
beautiful, and full of joy.
You are beautifully balanced.

Able to comfort, teach, and nourish others with My love.
I love the way you position your neck to fix your gaze on Me.
Your eyes are like deep reservoirs of adoration for Me.
They reflect great wisdom,
Which has brought you to a place of abundance
as a daughter of the King.
You still passionately cherish your salvation experience,
the day you became Mine.
Your mind is very pleasing to Me:
You've purposely programmed it with truth
and are vigilant to guard its thoughts.
You have allowed yourself to be intimate with Me.
This has created such glory all around you.
Even though I'm the King, I'm captivated by you.
You are decked in layers of beauty;
You are so sweet and pleasant to be around.
Oh, My love, I take exquisite pleasure in you!
Your upright, virtuous character bears much fruit;
Your compassionate nurturing of others
displays an abundance of desirable fruit.
I must sample this most desirable fruit,
the fruit of your works and walk,
the fruit of your compassionate nurturing.
I find your fruit abundant and most satisfying.
While sampling your fruit,
I noticed the sweet fragrance of life all around you.
The words you speak please Me.
They are beneficial for your welfare,
your prosperity, and your happiness.
They are just, fair, pleasant, and easy to receive.
Your words cause others to speak appropriately.

I am my Beloved's,
And He has convinced me that He desires me.
I am desirable.
Come, my beloved Bridegroom,
let us go where we can be alone with one another.
And when we must return to public places,
Let us choose a place that affords us easy access to alone time where we may be intimate.
Come with me to inspect the fruit of my soul and spirit.
In the deepest part of my soul, I long to know You.
In the hidden places of my spirit, I will love and worship You.
Notice the fragrance of our love,
Notice the fruit our love produces.
It enhances every area of our relationship,
And is most pleasant.
New fruit heaped upon the old.
I have hidden fruit for only You to behold and partake of,
my Beloved."

Reflection and Response

If you are doing this as a group Bible study, use day five as the day you come together. Go over the refection questions from each day together. Share, encourage, and pray for one another.

_____

_____

_____

If you are doing this study on your own, review the reflection and response sections from each day. Worship Him, and ask Him to do an even deeper work within you. Ask Him to add another layer of truth and beauty to your heart. Afterward, record your experience with Him.

WEEK NINE

Song of Solomon 8:1–2

SPIRITUAL INTIMACY

*A*s I did with the other seven chapters, before turning to any commentaries or concordances, I read this chapter several times. While praying for understanding and revelation, I felt to divide the chapter into two parts. This was not because of the length of the chapter, but because the subject matter changes drastically in the second half of the chapter. This week will cover verses 1–7.

VERSE 1:
"O that thou wert as my brother, that sucked the breasts of my mother!
When I should find thee without, I would kiss thee;
Yea, I should not be despised."

This is the bride talking to her bridegroom. This symbolizes you (or me) talking to Jesus, our Beloved. At first, I wondered why she would want her bridegroom to be like her younger brother. I believe it is so that she would feel no embarrassment or self-consciousness when showing affection for Him in public. Every keyword (brother, sucked, breasts, mother, without, kiss) means exactly what it says. The word *despised* means "to be shown contempt, to be scorned." It's true that when we are in public, our affections for Him are misunderstood, even scorned. My translation of verse 1:

KJV	MY VERSION
"O that thou wert as my brother, that sucked the breasts of my mother! When I should find thee without, I would kiss thee; Yea, I should not be despised."	"I wish I could openly show my affections for You in public as I would be able to if You were my little brother. Then I would avoid the scornful disrespect of others when I show my love for You."

VERSE 2:

"I would lead thee, and bring thee into my mother's house, who would instruct me: I would cause thee to drink of spiced wine of the juice of my pomegranate."

She is continuing to imagine how she could treat Him if He were her little brother. She could invite Him to her house without consideration for the judgmental thoughts of others. It almost reads like her mother will instruct her. However, renowned commentator Matthew Henry writes that the phrase "who would instruct me" refers back to the word *thee*, which refers to the bridegroom. She looks to her bridegroom for instruction and teaching.

The pomegranate is a sensual fruit that one would feed their lover. In chapter 1 we learned that His love for her is better than wine. Wine is associated with love. She loves Him and entertains Him with her love. Her love is spicy or passionate. This is a very sensual picture that symbolizes intimate worship, devotion, and prayer. Following is my presentation of verse 2:

KJV	MY VERSION
"I would lead thee, and bring thee into my mother's house, who would instruct me: I would cause thee to drink of spiced wine of the juice of my pomegranate."	"If You were like my little brother, I could bring You to my mother's house, where You could teach me, and where I could worship and love You with abandonment."

She desires to be with Him and express her love to Him. It's your turn now. Express your love to Him as you reread my rendition of these verses.

Reflections

Regarding intimacy with Jesus, to what extent do you hold back when you are in public?

_____
_____
_____
_____
_____

When is the appropriate time to be intimate with Jesus and hold back nothing?

Response

Press into His presence, and worship Him with abandonment. Unabashedly love on Him as if He were your baby brother. Record your experience with Him here.

WEEK NINE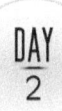

Song of Solomon 8:3–4

REST IN HIS EMBRACE

Unabashed, deeply sincere worship will often lead to what is described in these verses. The words from this verse are also found in chapter 2:6.

VERSE 3:
**"His left hand should be under my head,
and his right hand embraces me."**

This is a picture of intimacy. It is a picture of trust, rest, and contentment. The Lord desires spiritual intimacy with us. He wants us to rest in His love for us. He wants us to feel loved, safe, and content. Coming into His rest is realizing that we do not have to do or be anything to please Him. He did everything necessary so that we could rest in Him. It has been said that *intimacy* can be reworded to clarify its meaning as "into me see." It's to rest in Him, knowing that He sees absolutely everything about you, yet still embraces you and loves you completely. My rendering of verse 3:

KJV	MY VERSION
"His left hand should be under my head, and his right hand embraces me."	"His left hand is under my head, He knows all my thoughts, my very heart, His right hand embraces me, And I am at rest and safe in His love."

VERSE 4:
"I charge you, O daughters of Jerusalem, that ye stir not up, nor awake my love until he please."

He is asleep in her arms. She does not want anything or anyone to interrupt this rest she has found in him. *Jerusalem* means "the teaching of peace." She has found real peace. That's what we can find when we let Jesus teach us and become intimate with the Teacher, the Prince of Peace. She commands that everyone be still and quiet, especially the daughters of Jerusalem. She is with the bridegroom and charges the others not to disturb them. She does not want the moment to end. Even her thoughts, heart, and mind must be still and quiet. This is how it feels to be in His manifest presence. This is how it feels to be overcome by His love. You don't want it to end. His embrace supports us and keeps us from fainting in difficult times. Here is my rendition of verse 4:

KJV	MY VERSION
"I charge you, O daughters of Jerusalem, that ye stir not up, nor awake my love, until he please."	"I command anyone or anything that would disturb this incredible peace to be still and quiet. Do not disturb this moment of rest between my Love and myself. He is giving me strength to go on in this difficult time."

Please reread my translation of these verses, and realize that encounters with Him strengthen us for what is ahead. Don't neglect to let Him hold you, love on you, and strengthen you. He wants to with all His heart.

Reflections

Tell about a time you felt His embrace.

_____

_____

_____

Describe how that embrace gave you strength and why you needed it?

_____

_____

Response

Worship Jesus and ask Him to hold you. Ask Him to impart strength and knowledge that will carry you through the next season. Afterward, record your encounter with Him here.

_____

_____

_____

_____

_____

_____

_____

_____

_____

_____

_____

_____

WEEK NINE

Song of Solomon 8:5

OUT OF THE WILDERNESS

The scene now changes. It goes from a restful love scene in verse 4 to a picture of someone coming out of the wilderness. Let's see if we can figure out what's going on.

VERSE 5:
"Who is this that comes up out of the wilderness, leaning on her beloved? I raised thee up under the apple tree: There thy mother brought thee forth: There she brought thee forth that bare thee."

Recall verse 4: the daughters of Jerusalem were charged by the bride not to disturb her love. In the first part of verse 5, the daughters of Jerusalem ask her a question. It's almost like asking, "Who do you think you are?" After hearing the question, I can imagine the bride turning to Him and wondering who she is now. Upon reflection, she hardly recognizes herself. She is amazed at the spiritual progress she has made. And she knows it's because He has supported her and given her the strength needed to continue. He even carried her at times. I believe she looked to Him for the answer to the daughters' question because when He answered, He directed the answer to her instead of the daughters. He, the bridegroom, answers her. "I raised you up." *Raised* means "to exalt." He exalted her under the apple tree. The apple tree refers to chapter 2:3, where she compares Him to the shade of an apple tree. We learned in chapter 2 of this book that the apple tree is symbolic of the cross. She sat down under the shade of the cross; she accepted Jesus as her Savior. Song of Solomon 8:5 indicates that she was born under this apple tree. When we accept Christ as our Savior, we are born again of the Spirit as referred in John 3:5–8. The Holy Spirit would be the mother that is referred to in Song of Solomon 8:5. The Holy Spirit is the One who labors over our lives, bringing us to a place where we accept Him as our Savior and then raises us up or trains us in His ways.

This is my presentation of verse 5. First, the daughters of Jerusalem ask a question. Then the bride asks a question, then Christ answers. Let the words touch your heart.

KJV	MY VERSION
"Who is this that comes up out of the wilderness, leaning on her beloved? I raised thee up under the apple tree: There thy mother brought thee forth: There she brought thee forth that bare thee."	"Who is this, coming out of a hard season, leaning on her Beloved? Who am I? That You carried me and brought me out of the wilderness? *You, beloved, are the one I saved when you trusted in Me at the cross where you were born again of the Spirit, Who labored over you with love.*"

This describes our journey. It begins at the cross, progresses to intimacy with the Savior, Who (along with Holy Spirit) brings us through the good times and the hard times. He labors over us, teaches us, strengthens us, and leads us. We are His, and He is faithful to be with us on every step of our journey. He will never leave us or forsake us. Please read my rendition of verse 5 once again.

Reflections

Think about a hard season of your life. Can you look back and find Jesus? What was He doing?

_____

_____

_____

What does the "apple tree" refer to?

_____

_____

_____

Who does your "mother" refer to in this verse?

_____

_____

_____

Response

Worship Him for being with you every step of the way. Thank Him for carrying you when you had no strength. Thank Him for imparting strength, teaching you, leading you, and for not forsaking you. Afterward, record how your time with Him impacted you.

_____

_____

_____

_____

_____

_____

_____

_____

_____

_____

_____

_____

WEEK NINE

Song of Solomon 8:6–7

VOWS

It's hard to determine who is speaking in verse 6. Some commentaries state that it is the bride but also admit it could be the groom. I feel it could be either. As I studied and prayed, I realized that it is both. I will explain my thoughts.

VERSE 6:
"Set me as a seal upon thine heart, as a seal upon thine arm:
For love is strong as death; Jealousy as cruel as the grave:
The coals thereof are coals of fire, which have a most vehement flame."

Set means "establish, appoint, or fix." *Seal* refers to a signet ring. A signet ring is a ring with an engraving made of clay that leaves an impression on documents or other surfaces. Exodus 28:11 tells us that the names of the children of Israel were engraved on a stone as a signet. This stone was worn as a breastplate by the high priest. Check out Isaiah 49:16—you are engraved on His hands. I love that!

The thought of setting (establishing, appointing, fixing) their relationship, combined with the engraved ring, makes this passage feel like a wedding charge, or like vows each speaks to the other.

The bride requests, "Let me always have a place in your heart, let me make an impression of love upon your heart." Perhaps the bridegroom is responding, "Beloved, I have made you a signet, engraving your name upon my breast and my hand. Let me always have a place in your heart, let me make an impression of love upon your heart."

They each declare their love is as *strong* (mighty, fierce) as death. Christ's love for us is as strong as death. His love defeated death for us. Many Bible verses declare Christ's resurrection and victory over death. 2 Timothy 1:10 is one example.

The love of a true believer for Christ is a strong as death, for it makes them dead to everything else. Jesus said, "If any man will come after me, let him deny himself, and take up his cross, and follow me. For whosoever will save his life shall lose it: and whosoever will lose his life for my sake shall find it" (Matthew 16:24–25).

Their love is so strong that it evokes "jealousy as cruel as the grave." *Cruel* refers to "intensity, such as rigorous as a battle." *Grave* followed by *coals of fire* implies hell. Their love produces cruel, intense jealousy, which is comparable to a battlefield or to the fires of hell itself. The coals of their love are as the coals of fire. This speaks of burning, of insatiable desire, of unquenchable passion for one another. *Strong's Concordance* says that *fire* as used in this verse is a supernatural fire. *Vehement* is defined as "forceful, intense, and passionate." Here is my translation of verse 6. It allows for the bride and bridegroom to speak certain parts of the verse as if repeating them back to the other.

KJV	MY VERSION
"Set me as a seal upon thine heart, as a seal upon thine arm: For love is strong as death; Jealousy as cruel as the grave: The coals thereof are coals of fire, which have a most vehement flame."	*"Let My love make an impression upon your heart, May that impression be so deep and personal that nothing but My love can fill it. Our love is as strong as death. My love for you is great. I died for you, My beloved.* Let My love make an impression upon Your heart, May that impression be so deep and personal that nothing but my love can fill it. Our love is as strong as death. My love for you is great. I die to the things the world offers me. I separate myself to You and You alone. Our love is intensely jealous of other lovers and is as passionate as flames of fire. *Yes, our love is intensely jealous of other lovers and is as passionate as flames of fire."*

VERSE 7:
"Many waters cannot quench love, neither can the floods drown it:
If a man would give all of the substance of his house for love,
It would be utterly contemned."

  Many waters refers to the damage and violence of an abundance of water, which points to trials and tribulations. These "cannot quench" (extinguish or overcome) our love. Even a *flood* (rushing, running waters) cannot drown or sweep our love away. His love for us is invincible. Because of His love for us, "Christ waded through great difficulties, even seas of blood" (Henry). A man giving "all the substance of his house" can be translated as a man giving up all his wealth and riches. The sum of that wealth would not be enough, it would be "utterly contemned" or considered insignificant compared to the value of their love. In other words, a value cannot be placed on love such as this. It's hard to determine who is saying this, whether it is the bride or the groom. I would like to continue reading it as part of their vows to one another, each in turn expressing the value of the other's love.

KJV	MY VERSION
"Many waters cannot quench love, neither can the floods drown it: If a man would give all of the substance of his house for love, It would be utterly contemned."	*"An abundance of violence and blood did not alter My love for you.* Your love is more valuable to me than all the wealth and riches this world offers."

To me, these beautiful verses seem like wedding vows, or possibly engagement vows. Please reread them with Jesus.

Reflections

To what degree is your love for Jesus as strong as death?

_____

_____

To what degree is your love for Jesus as passionate as flames of fire?

Response

Spend some time with Jesus. Let Him hear your vows of love. Listen as He declares and vows His love for you. Record what He says to you.

WEEK NINE

Song of Solomon 8:1–7
INTIMACY

*H*ere is my presentation of Song of Solomon, chapter 8:1–7, with the symbolism and metaphors replaced for greater understanding. When you get down to the vows, read your part to Him (plain script), love on Him, and let Him love on you (italics):

"I wish I could openly show my affections for You in public
as I would be able to if You were my little brother.
Then I would avoid the scornful disrespect of others
when I show my love for You.
If You were like my little brother,
I could bring You to my mother's house,
where You could teach me, and where I could worship
and love You with abandonment.
*His left hand is under my head,
He knows all my thoughts, my very heart,
His right hand embraces me,
and I am at rest and safe in His love.*

I command anyone or anything
that would disturb this incredible peace to be still and quiet.
Do not disturb this moment of rest between my Love and myself.
He is giving me strength to go on in this difficult time.
Who is this coming out of a hard season, leaning on her Beloved?
Who am I? That You carried me and brought me out of the wilderness?
You, beloved, are the one I saved when you trusted in Me at the cross,
where you were born again of the Spirit, Who labored over you with love.
Let My love make an impression upon your heart.
May that impression be so deep and personal
that nothing but My love can fill it.
Our love is as strong as death.
My love for you is great. I died for you, My beloved.
Let My love make an impression upon Your heart,
May that impression be so deep and personal
that nothing but my love can fill it.
Our love is as strong as death. My love for You is great.
I die to the things the world offers me.
I separate myself to You and You alone.
Our love is intensely jealous of other lovers
and is as passionate as flames of fire.
Yes, our love is intensely jealous of other lovers
and is as passionate as flames of fire.
An abundance of violence and blood
did not alter My love for you.
Your love is more valuable to me
than all the wealth and riches this world offers."

Reflection and Response

If you are doing this as a group Bible study, use day five as the day you come together. Go over the refection questions from each day together. Share, encourage, and pray for one another.

_____

_____

_____

_____

_____

If you are doing this study on your own, review the reflection and response sections from each day. Worship Him and ask Him to do an even deeper work. Ask Him to add another layer of truth and beauty to your heart. Afterward, record your experience with Him.

_____

_____

_____

_____

_____

WEEK TEN

Song of Solomon 8:8–9

THE LOST

As husbands often do, Jesus must have shared His plans to include the Gentiles as part of the church. The wife responds to His plans by asking her husband a question.

<u>**VERSE 8:**</u>
"We have a little sister, and she hath no breasts:
What shall we do for our sister in the day when she shall be spoken for?"

The sister is symbolic of the Gentile church. The passage is best understood as the Jewish church showing concern for the Gentile church. She sees the Gentile church as having no breasts, meaning "untaught, unfed, or unnourished spiritually." The Gentiles had neither the Word nor the opportunity for grace. She is concerned about how this deficiency in them will be supplied (Wesley). On a personal level, we would apply this as showing concern for the lost. Our Bridegroom's mission is "to seek and save the lost" (Luke 19:10). Here is my interpretation of verse 8:

KJV	MY VERSION
"We have a little sister, and she hath no breasts: What shall we do for our sister in the day when she shall be spoken for?"	"You have shown me Your plan to extend Your love to the lost, but they have never known You, Your love or Your Word. How will they ever be equipped?"

VERSE 9:

"If she be a wall, we will build upon her a palace of silver: And if she be a door, we will enclose her with boards of cedar."

Jesus answers His bride's question by laying out two scenarios for individuals at the time of their salvation. *Wall* is symbolic of one who is strong in their faith. This new believer has the foundation to become a palace of silver. The Bridegroom says to His bride, "We will build upon her . . ." (upon this foundation). We includes the Father, Son, and Holy Spirit, as well as the church, His espoused bride. Becoming a "palace of silver" indicates significant growth and extreme value. *Palace* can mean "battlement, an impenetrable fortress" that the enemy cannot easily destroy.

The second scenario involves the new convert being compared to a door. *Door* refers to an easily accessible woman. It means that the person is pretty much open to anything and points to weak faith. The solution is that we, the same Father, Son, Holy Spirit, and church, will enclose the new convert. *Enclose* means "to secure, strengthen and fortify" their faith. Their faith will be strengthened and fortified with cedar, which is a sweet-smelling wood that is very strong and durable, one that does not rot easily or quickly. Cedar was used in purification rituals and cleansings. This signifies the spiritual cleansing that a person often needs. Here's my presentation of verse 9:

KJV	MY VERSION
"If she be a wall, we will build upon her a palace of silver: And if she be a door, we will enclose her with boards of cedar."	*"If her faith in Me is strong, My Father, the Holy Spirit, Myself, and you will team up together adding to the foundation of her faith. She will become a strong, valuable fortress for Me. If her faith in Me is weak leaving her open to the enemies' strategies, My Father, the Holy Spirit, Myself, and you will team up together fortifying her faith until she has been cleansed, and becomes strong and durable."*

Wow, I love this. When we say yes to His love, we become aware of His heart, which is to seek and save the lost (Luke 19:10). His mission becomes our mission. He shares His plans with us, and we get to help Him carry them out. Please reread my rendition of verses 8 and 9.

Reflections

To what degree do you have a burden for the lost?

_____
_____
_____

Make a list of those that come to your mind. Ask Jesus to show you how to pray for them. Ask Him for opportunities to speak to them about His love.

Response

Spend some time with your Savior, praying for those He has placed on your heart.

WEEK TEN

Song of Solomon 8:10

FAVORED

The bride is speaking in this verse. She is addressing her little sister, encouraging her, expressing her confidence in the work of grace He has planned for her.

VERSE 10:
"I am a wall and my breasts like towers:
Then was I in his eyes as one that found favor."

The bride attributes her growth and strength to His steadfast love and nurturing. She declares that she has become a wall, a strong valuable fortress. Her "breasts like towers" symbolize spiritual growth, maturity, and strength. She comforts little sister, acknowledging that it was Jesus who accomplished this in her and will do it for little sister as well.

Found means "to attain." Her yielding to His work of grace has allowed her to find, attain, lay hold of, or secure favor. *Favor* indicates "completeness, soundness, safety, welfare, health, prosperity, peace, and contentment." My rendition of verse 10 looks like this:

KJV	MY VERSION
"I am a wall and my breasts like towers: Then was I in his eyes as one that found favor."	"New believer, consider me: Due to His love and commitment to nurture me, I have fully matured in strength and value. By yielding to the work of His grace, I have become complete. In Him, I am sound, safe, well, healthy, prosperous, peaceful, and content."

Read verse 10 again and declare those words of truth about yourself.

Reflections

Describe the work of His grace in your life.

_____
_____
_____

To what extent do these words describe you: sound, safe, well, healthy, prosperous, peaceful, and content?

_____
_____
_____

Response

Worship Him for the work of grace. Talk to Him about any concerns you express in the above reflection. Write down His response, and record your experience with Him.

_____

_____

_____

_____

_____

_____

_____

_____

_____

_____

_____

_____

_____

_____

WEEK TEN

Song of Solomon 8:11–13
KEEPER OF THE VINEYARD

Bible commentaries were necessary for me to tap into the meaning of this verse. When we finish, it will make sense and apply to us. Yay, I like that.

VERSE 11:
"Solomon had a vineyard at Baal-Hamon;
He let out the vineyard unto keepers;
Every one for the fruit thereof was to bring
a thousand pieces of silver."

Solomon trusted keepers to see to the needs of his vineyard. The keepers were to bring the profits from the fruit to Solomon. *Baal-Hamon* means "to rule a crowd." *Solomon* is an Old Testament type and shadow of Christ. One of Christ's names is the Prince of Peace (Isaiah 9:6). Compare that to Solomon's name, which means "peace." *Vineyard* is symbolic of the church and can also symbolize the human heart or spirit.

Each individual is responsible for the condition of their own heart; they must keep their own vineyard and tend the fruit it is producing. They must give all the glory to Jesus for their good fruit, not taking any credit themselves. Bringing the thousand pieces of silver to the vineyard's owner is a picture of giving all the glory to Christ. "Just as Solomon ruled over the orchard which he owned, having purchased it with revenue, so Christ has purchased us with His blood and should rule over us or become our Lord" (Wesley). I present my rendition of verse 11:

KJV	MY VERSION
"Solomon had a vineyard at Baal-Hamon; He let out the vineyard unto keepers; Every one for the fruit thereof was to bring a thousand pieces of silver."	*"Yes, my Beloved, in Me you are complete, sound, safe, healthy, prosperous, peaceful, and content. Your spirit is My garden, but you, My beloved, are responsible for its condition; Remember that the fruit your spirit produces is Mine. All the glory is Mine."*

VERSE 12:
"My vineyard, which is mine, is before me: Thou, O Solomon, must have a thousand, And those that keep the fruit thereof two hundred."

The bride is responding to the charge, from verse 11, saying that she is responsible for the condition of the vineyard, her spirit. In Song of Solomon 1:6, the bride confesses to neglecting her own vineyard. Here she declares that her vineyard is always uppermost in her mind or "is before me." She admits that all of the fruit, "a thousand," is rightfully

His (Christ's), but she recognizes that she benefits "two hundred" from keeping her vineyard.

Our work is to keep (maintain and guard) our heart, our spirit. Solomon penned, "Keep thy heart with all diligence; for out of it are the issues of life" (Proverbs 4:23). Think about Adam in the book of Genesis. He was to keep of the Garden of Eden so that God could take pleasure in walking in it. Below is my interpretation of verse 12:

KJV	MY VERSION
"My vineyard, which is mine, is before me: Thou, O Solomon, must have a thousand, And those that keep the fruit thereof two hundred."	"I diligently maintain and guard my spirit; I honor all the good You have done in me; I give You all the glory; but I, too, benefit greatly from giving attention to the condition of my spirit."

VERSE 13:
"Thou that dwellest in the gardens,
the companions harken unto thy voice:
Cause me to hear it."

The one who lives in our garden (or spirit) is Christ. We should develop a close relationship with Him like we would a friend. We should be able to hear His voice speaking to us. We should recognize His voice. Until we begin to recognize His voice, we cannot "harken" to it or obey Him. We need to develop that hearing ear (John 19:27).

Jesus said, "If any man has ears to hear, let him hear" (Matthew 13:9, 43). He often said this about understanding His parables. *Ears* is a metaphor pointing to the faculty of perceiving in the mind, the faculty of understanding and knowing. It is one thing to hear His words but another to understand their meaning. The word *hear* in Song of Solomon 8 means "to hear, to listen, and to obey." Most often, when Jesus spoke the word *hear*, it translates as "to understand or perceive." We are called not only to hear but also to understand so that we can obey. I spent many years praying that I would "have ears to hear," to truly hear and understand Christ's written Word as well as what He speaks to my heart. That's what the bride in Song of Solomon is praying. She is praying to hear and understand His voice so that she can obey it. My interpretation of verse 13 is as follows:

KJV	MY VERSION
"Thou that dwellest in the gardens, the companions harken unto thy voice: Cause me to hear it."	"You live in my spirit; I should be able to hear Your voice. Your friends recognize and obey Your voice. Oh, how I want to hear, recognize, and obey Your voice. Help me hear."

Before I leave verse 13 with her prayer for hearing ears, I want to make a connection to verses 9 and 10. In those verses, we found that we have a part in discipling new believers. We are trusted with the privilege of co-laboring with the Father, Son, and Holy Spirit. For us to complement the work of the Godhead, we must be able to hear what is being said about each individual. Only God truly knows a person's heart, what they have gone through, and what His plans are for them. We must learn to tune into His voice as we co-labor with Him. Please reread my rendition of verses 11–13.

Reflections

Who is responsible for the condition of your heart?

_____

_____

_____

_____

Who gets the glory for what is right and good in your heart?

_____

_____

_____

_____

How do you benefit from the attention you give to keeping your heart?

_____

_____

_____

_____

Response

Press into His presence. Tell Him that you long to know and hear His voice. Record what He says.

WEEK TEN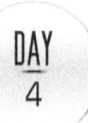

Song of Solomon 8:14

LONGING FOR HIS RETURN

We have arrived at the very last verse of this great romantic book. The key to this verse is to identify who is speaking.

VERSE 14:
"Make haste, my beloved, and be thou like to a row or to a young hart upon the mountains of spices."

The word *beloved* refers to a male lover. This brings clarity concerning who is speaking. The bride is speaking to the bridegroom, asking Him to "hasten," or "come quickly." She compares Him to a roe or a hart. *Hart* can also be translated as a ram. Both belong to the deer family. Both are known for their beauty, glory, honor, and prominence. They are also known for their sure-footedness and ability to move quickly over the mountains. The *mountains* refer to the heavens.

The *spices* are a sweet smell or a sweet odor. This fragrance refers to the incense being stored up in heaven, which is the essence of the accumulation of the prayers of all the saints through the ages. In Revelation 8:3–4, we are told this incense will be released right before the return of Christ. Check out this dialog from Revelation:

"And the Spirit and the bride say, Come." (Revelation 22:17)
Jesus answers; "Surely I come quickly." (Revelation 22:20)
We reply: *"Amen. Even so, come Lord Jesus."* (Revelation 22:20)

Even though He lives in our hearts, talks to us, walks with us, and never leaves us, we are ever aware that He is not with us bodily. The more intimate we become with Him, the more we will yearn for His return. The day that He comes for His bride, to claim us as His own, to rapture our souls up to heaven where we will no longer be apart from Him in any sense of the word will be a glorious day. Here is my interpretation of verse 14:

KJV	MY VERSION
"Make haste, my beloved, and be thou like to a row or to a young hart upon the mountains of spices."	"Come quickly, My beloved Jesus, Come swiftly in all Your beauty and glory and honor and prominence. When You break through the heavens, returning for us, the very fragrance of heaven will be released, All our prayers will be answered in Your coming."

Reflections

To what extent do you long for His return? Do you hope that He delays His return? Why? Be specific.

_____
_____
_____
_____

Response

I find that when I press into His presence and express my longing for His return, I am quickly reminded of the lost and their need for Him. I am also reminded of my responsibility to pray for them and reach out to them. That is my response. Press into His presence and record your insights here:

_____
_____
_____
_____

WEEK TEN

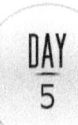

Song of Solomon 8

THE MATURE

I felt called to title this portion of chapter 8 The Mature. Only the mature will notice the spiritual needs and deficiencies of others. Only the mature will work in yielded cooperation with the Father, Son, and Holy Spirit to supply what is needed. Only the mature will truly listen to, understand, and obey the instructions written and spoken by the Godhead. Only the mature will carefully apply those instructions to her own heart, as well as make them known to others. Only the mature long dearly for His return and grieve His bodily absence. Now enjoy my rendition Song of Solomon 8 in its entirety:

> "I wish I could openly show my affections for You in public
> as I would be able to if You were my little brother.
> Then I would avoid the scornful disrespect of others
> when I show my love for You.
> If You were like my little brother,
> I could bring You to my mother's house,
> Where You could teach me,
> and where I could worship and love You with abandonment.

His left hand is under my head,
He knows all my thoughts, my very heart,
His right-hand embraces me, I am at rest and safe in His love.
I command anyone or anything that would disturb
this incredible peace to be still, to be quiet.
Do not disturb this moment of rest between my Love and I.
He is giving me strength to go on in this difficult time.
Who is this coming out of a hard season, leaning on her Beloved?
Who am I?
That You carried me and brought me out of the wilderness?
*You, beloved, are the one I saved when you trusted in Me at the cross,
where you were born again of the Spirit, Who labored over you with love.
Let My love make an impression upon your heart.
May that impression be so deep and personal
that nothing but My love can fill it.
Our love is as strong as death. My love for you is great.
I died for you, My beloved.*
Let my love make an impression upon Your heart.
May that impression be so deep and personal
that nothing but my love can fill it.
Our love is as strong as death. My love for You is great.
I die to the things the world offers me.
I separate myself to You and You alone.
Our love is intensely jealous of other lovers
and is as passionate as flames of fire.
*Yes, our love is intensely jealous of other lovers
and is as passionate as flames of fire.
An abundance of violence and blood did not alter My love for you.*
Your love is more valuable to me
than all the wealth and riches this world offers.
You have shown me Your plan to extend Your love to the lost,
but they have never known You, Your love or Your word.

How will they ever be equipped?
If her faith in Me is strong,
My Father, the Holy Spirit, Myself, and you will team up together
adding to the foundation of her faith.
She will become a strong, valuable fortress for Me.
If her faith in Me is weak, leaving her open to the enemies' strategies,
My Father, the Holy Spirit, Myself, and you will team up together
fortifying her faith until she has been cleansed,
and becomes strong and durable.
New believer, consider me:
Due to His love and commitment to nurture me,
I have fully matured in strength and value.
By yielding to the work of His grace, I have become complete.
In Him, I am sound, safe, well,
healthy, prosperous, peaceful, and content.
Yes, My beloved, in Me you are complete, sound, safe, well,
healthy, prosperous, peaceful, and content.
Your spirit is My garden,
but you, My beloved, are responsible for its condition;
remember that the fruit your spirit produces is Mine.
All the glory is Mine.
I diligently maintain and guard my spirit;
I honor all the good You have done in me;
I give You all the glory;
but I too benefit greatly from giving attention
to the condition of my spirit.
You live in my spirit; I should be able to hear Your voice.
Your friends recognize and obey Your voice.
Oh, how I want to hear, recognize and obey Your voice.
Help me hear.
Come quickly, My beloved Jesus,

> Come swiftly in all Your beauty and glory
> and honor and prominence.
> When You break through the heavens, returning for us,
> the very fragrance of heaven will be released,
> All our prayers will be answered in Your coming."

Wow, we're all done. I'm crying as I write this paragraph. I can't tell you what a blessing it has been to explore this glorious book and share the wonderful, life-changing truths with you. My prayer is that, in reading and journaling through these pages, you have become more intimate with Jesus, the lover of your soul, and that your relationship with Him continues to deepen.

Reflection and Response

If you are doing this as a group Bible study, use day five as the day you come together. Go over the refection questions from each day together. Share, encourage, and pray for one another.

_____

_____

_____

_____

_____

If you are doing this study on your own, review the reflection and response sections from each day. Worship Him, and ask Him to do an even deeper work in you. Ask Him to add another layer of truth and beauty to your heart. Afterward, record your experience with Him here.

_____

_____

_____

_____

_____

CONCLUSION

THE SONG OF ALL SONGS

As I prayerfully considered a conclusion for this book, several thoughts surfaced. Solomon introduced his writing as the "the song of songs," indicating that it was and is the best song ever written or sung because it is a song of love between himself and his bride. Our studies uncovered all the symbolism, poetic imagery, metaphors, and allegories to discover that the song is a picture of each individual love story with Jesus, our soon-to-be Bridegroom. It shows the progression and deepening of love that is possible with our Savior.

I encourage you to prayerfully consider the depth of your relationship with Jesus. Ask Him which chapter represents where you are now in your walk with Him. Keep in mind that the work of the Lord in our lives happens in layers. You may find yourself revisiting some chapters that you thought where behind you. Don't fret over this. He is simply doing a deeper work and adding another layer of beauty and strength to your life. Embrace His love. Let Him sing this song over you. It is an eternal song that never ends. He knew you and loved you before your conception (Psalm 139). He loves you now, and He will love you for all of eternity. His song surrounds you (Psalm 32:7). Stop and listen to Him sing over you.

I love you, my friends. I truly do. You allowed me to share my heart with you and I truly love you for it.

www.ingramcontent.com/pod-product-compliance
Lightning Source LLC
Chambersburg PA
CBHW030318100526
44592CB00010B/475